The ADHD Chronicles

A Compassionate Guide to ADHD
Management, Unleashing Potential, and
Nurturing Resilience in Your Child's
Journey

Christy J. Hall

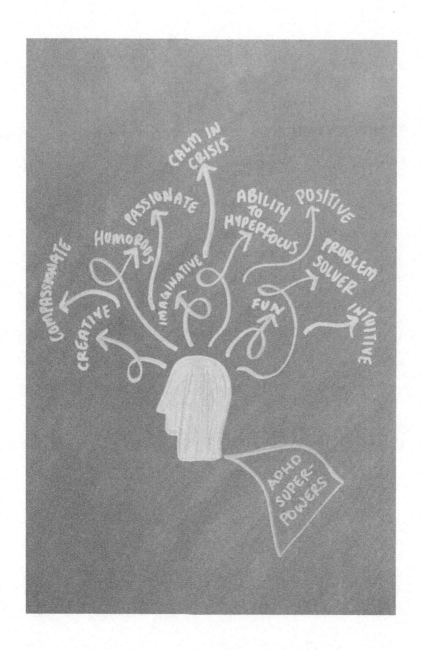

TABLE OF CONTENTS

Introduction

Defining ADHD

Attention Deficit Hyperactivity illness (ADHD) is a neurodevelopmental illness that is defined by persistent patterns of inattention, impulsivity, and hyperactivity that severely interfere with a person's everyday functioning or development. This disorder is also known as attention deficit hyperactivity disorder. The symptoms often appear throughout infancy, and they may last into puberty and sometimes even into maturity. Recognizing the multidimensional nature of attention-deficit/hyperactivity disorder (ADHD) and its influence on numerous elements of an individual's life is necessary for understanding the condition.

Treatment and Management:

Behavioral Therapy: Strategies concentrating on positive reinforcement, organization, and social skills might be effective.

Medication: In certain circumstances, healthcare providers may prescribe stimulant or non-stimulant drugs to control symptoms.

Understanding ADHD demands a comprehensive view, understanding the various experiences of those impacted by the illness. A coordinated approach including parents, educators, and healthcare experts is critical for successful intervention and support. It's crucial to tackle ADHD with empathy, identifying the different ways in which it presents itself, and adapting therapies to fit the particular needs of people afflicted.

Recognizing Symptoms and Types

In this chapter, we go into the important parts of detecting and comprehending the symptoms and kinds of attention deficit hyperactivity disorder (ADHD). By gaining insight into the different ways ADHD may appear, readers will be better able to spot possible difficulties in youngsters. The important components of this chapter include:

Inattentiveness: Detailed investigation of inattentive symptoms, such as trouble maintaining concentration, making casual errors, and forgetting.

Real-life situations exhibit how inattentiveness may affect academic achievement and everyday activities.

Hyperactivity: A comprehensive discussion on hyperactive symptoms, including excessive fidgeting, restlessness, and difficulty remaining sat.

Behavioral examples showcasing hyperactivity in many circumstances, from the classroom to social environments.

Being impulsive: In-depth investigation of impulsive behaviors, such as difficulties waiting one's time, interrupting others, and hasty decision-making.

Insights into how impulsivity may affect relationships, academic work, and personal growth.

Subtypes of ADHD:

A thorough discussion of the three primary subtypes— Predominantly Inattentive, Predominantly Hyperactive-Impulsive, and Combined Presentation.

Case studies and stories to assist readers in identifying traits connected with each category.

Developmental Considerations: Recognition of how ADHD symptoms may appear differently at various stages of development, highlighting the significance of age-appropriate testing.

Assessment Tools: Overview of frequently used assessment methods and questionnaires for diagnosing ADHD symptoms.

Guidance on getting expert aid for a full diagnosis.

Importance of Early Intervention

Early intervention in attention deficit hyperactivity disorder (ADHD) is crucial for various reasons, each contributing to the overall well-being and success of the child. Understanding the relevance of timely action may dramatically alter the direction of a child's life:

Neurodevelopmental Plasticity: The early years of life are defined by heightened neuroplasticity, where the brain is more malleable to change and learning. Early intervention makes use of this key era to create beneficial brain connections.

Academic Success: Early detection and intervention boost a child's chances of academic achievement. Addressing ADHD-related issues in learning early on helps avert academic failures and pave the path for a more favorable school experience.

Social and Emotional Well-being: Social and emotional development is directly connected to early intervention. By treating ADHD-related issues in social interactions and emotional control early, children may create stronger connections and a more solid emotional foundation.

Preventing Secondary Issues: Timely care can avoid or decrease subsequent obstacles associated with untreated ADHD, such as behavioral disorders, poor self-esteem, and academic underachievement. It pauses the potential negative cycle that might emerge without sufficient assistance.

Family Dynamics: Early intervention favorably improves family relations. By offering assistance and methods for parents and caregivers, the family becomes better able to recognize and handle ADHD-related difficulties, establishing a more supportive atmosphere.

Community and Educational Systems: Collaborative initiatives between schools, communities, and healthcare professionals are more successful when undertaken early. Creating ADHD-friendly surroundings and adopting adjustments early on may significantly affect a child's educational trajectory.

Long-Term Prognosis: Research shows that people who get early care for ADHD frequently demonstrate superior long-term results. Early assistance may lead to stronger coping skills, enhanced resilience, and a better overall prognosis.

Challenges & Barriers: Acknowledging possible problems and limitations to early action is key. Identifying and overcoming these hurdles ensures that children get the essential assistance in a timely way, enhancing the efficacy of treatments.

Understanding the significance of early intervention allows parents, educators, and healthcare professionals to take proactive actions in diagnosing and resolving ADHD in its early phases. By doing so, we may offer children with the skills they need to overcome the hurdles associated with ADHD, encouraging a route towards a more successful and meaningful future.

Chapter 1: Diagnosing ADHD

Pediatrician's Role

Pediatricians have a significant role in the diagnosis of attention deficit hyperactivity disorder (ADHD). Here's a quick overview:

Initial Evaluation: Conduct an initial evaluation based on parental and teacher reports, monitoring the child's behavior and developmental history.

Referral to Specialists: Refer families to professionals, such as child psychologists or psychiatrists, for a more in-depth examination when ADHD is suspected.

Collaboration with Parents: Work closely with parents to obtain information on the child's conduct at home and in other situations.

Use of Diagnostic Criteria: Apply diagnostic criteria, frequently from the DSM-5, to see whether the observed behaviors correspond with ADHD.

Consideration of Differential Diagnoses: Rule out other possible reasons for symptoms by thorough investigation of differential diagnosis.

Communication with School: Collaborate with instructors to obtain insights regarding the child's behavior and performance in an academic setting.

Monitoring and Follow-up: Monitor the child's development and, if identified, cooperate on a suitable treatment plan.

The doctor plays a crucial role in the earliest phases of ADHD diagnosis, working with other experts to achieve a full picture of the child's behavior and requirements.

Involvement of Psychologists and Specialists

Psychologists and experts are crucial to the diagnostic path of attention deficit hyperactivity disorder (ADHD), playing a vital role in understanding and resolving the complexity involved with this neurodevelopmental illness.

Comprehensive Assessment: At the basis of their engagement is the dedication to performing detailed evaluations. Going beyond surface-level observations, psychologists apply standardized instruments to examine cognitive function, attention span, and behavioral tendencies. This rigorous examination tries to develop a complete picture of the child's strengths and weaknesses, offering nuanced knowledge that leads to the diagnostic procedure.

Collaboration with Professionals: Psychologists and experts employ a collaborative approach by actively interacting with other professionals engaged in the child's care. This collaborative effort guarantees that the diagnostic process benefits from varied viewpoints and knowledge. Close coordination with physicians allows for a full review of the child's health history, examining any medical problems that may contribute to ADHD symptoms. Working closely with educators gives insights into the child's behavior in an academic setting, enhancing the diagnostic procedure with a larger context.

Differential Diagnosis: Meticulous attention is devoted to completing a differential diagnosis and understanding that ADHD symptoms might overlap with other illnesses. This includes ruling out alternate explanations for the observed behaviors and confirming the veracity of the diagnosis. Through careful evaluation and extra examinations where required, psychologists seek to separate ADHD from other possible factors, opening the way for more focused therapies.

Communication with Parents: Acknowledging the vital role parents play in understanding their child's behavior, psychologists actively seek assistance from parents. Open and collaborative talks give vital insights into family dynamics, developmental history, and the child's conduct at home. Parental involvement helps greatly to the accuracy of the diagnostic procedure, connecting the insights with the child's experiences in diverse situations.

Feedback to Educators: To incorporate clinical insights into the educational context, psychologists give constructive comments to educators. This facilitates a smooth translation of diagnostic results into the child's academic environment.

By assisting with tactics and adjustments that enhance academic performance, psychologists help to the creation of a supportive educational framework for children with ADHD.

In essence, psychologists and experts contribute experience, accuracy, and a collaborative attitude to the ADHD diagnosis process. Through extensive evaluations, collaborative initiatives, and the creation of specialized therapies, they contribute to a more precise knowledge of each child's specific situation, permitting focused assistance and solutions.

Criteria for ADHD Diagnosis

The diagnosis of attention deficit hyperactivity disorder (ADHD) is based on specific criteria stated in generally regarded diagnostic standards, such as the Diagnostic and Statistical Manual of Mental Disorders (DSM-5). These factors aid healthcare practitioners in effectively diagnosing and classifying persons with ADHD. The primary criteria for ADHD diagnosis include:

Symptom Presentation:

Inattention: A chronic pattern of inattention, marked by thoughtless errors, trouble maintaining attention, poor organization, and forgetfulness in everyday tasks.

Hyperactivity: Excessive fidgeting, restlessness, an inability to remain sat in settings when it is required, and frequent moving.

Impulsivity: Impulsive actions include interrupting others, difficulties waiting one's turn, and making fast judgments without contemplating the repercussions.

Duration and Severity:

The symptoms must be present for at least six months and be more frequent and severe than those found in persons at a similar developmental stage.

Onset Age:

Symptoms should show before the age of 12, suggesting that ADHD is a neurodevelopmental illness with origins in early childhood.

Functional Impairment:

The symptoms must cause severe impairment in social, academic, or vocational functioning. This impairment should be visible in two or more locations, such as at home, school, or in relationships.

Differential Diagnoses

When reviewing symptoms that may imply attention deficit hyperactivity disorder (ADHD), healthcare providers need to investigate and rule out other illnesses that may present with comparable characteristics. Differential diagnoses for ADHD include:

Learning Disorders: Conditions such as dyslexia or other learning impairments may appear as inattention or academic problems, warranting investigation throughout the diagnostic procedure.

Anxiety Disorders: Generalized anxiety disorder or social anxiety disorder may manifest with restlessness, trouble focusing, and irritability, overlapping with ADHD symptoms.

Mood Disorders: Conditions like depression or bipolar disease may entail fluctuations in energy levels, attention, and focus, leading to parallels with ADHD symptoms.

Autism Spectrum Disorders (ASD): Some aspects of ASD, notably difficulty with social interaction, communication, and repetitive behaviors, may be confused for ADHD symptoms, underscoring the need for a comprehensive examination.

Intellectual Disabilities: Individuals with intellectual impairments may demonstrate issues in attention and focus, needing careful consideration throughout the diagnosis procedure.

Sensory Processing Disorders: Sensory processing difficulties may contribute to distractibility and restlessness, reflecting ADHD symptoms. An examination of sensory processing is necessary to separate these disorders.

Oppositional Defiant Disorder (ODD) and Conduct Disorder (CD): Behavioral disorders like ODD and CD might overlap traits with ADHD, such as impulsivity and disobedience. A detailed assessment helps separate these disorders.

Sleep Disorders: Sleep disorders, such as sleep apnea or insomnia, may contribute to inattention, hyperactivity, and impulsivity, stressing the need to evaluate sleep patterns in the diagnosis process.

Medical Conditions: Certain medical problems, such as thyroid malfunction or lead poisoning, might impair cognitive function and behavior, resembling ADHD symptoms.

Giftedness: Highly talented people may demonstrate strong interests, hyperfocus, and restlessness, which may be misunderstood as ADHD. A grasp of intellectual giftedness is necessary for correct distinction.

Language Disorders: Abnormalities influencing language development, such as expressive or receptive language abnormalities, may lead to difficulty in communication and attention, needing extensive testing.

Tourette Syndrome: The existence of tics in Tourette Syndrome may lead to hyperactivity and impulsivity, needing care in the diagnosis process.

A complete examination, incorporating medical, psychological, and educational variables, is necessary for accurate differential diagnosis. Collaboration between healthcare experts, educators, and parents, combined with observations across numerous contexts, helps provide a complex picture of the individual's behavior and functioning. A rigorous elimination of these possible confounding variables assists in a more accurate diagnosis and the creation of suitable therapeutic methods.

Chapter 2: Behavioral Therapy and Parenting Strategies

Positive Reinforcement Techniques

Positive reinforcement is a beneficial strategy for parents controlling behaviors related to attention deficit hyperactivity disorder (ADHD). Here are excellent positive reinforcement approaches for parents:

Immediate and Specific Praise: Offer prompt and precise praise for desirable actions.

Clearly describe what behavior is being appreciated, creating a positive relationship.

Catch Them Being Good: Regularly notice and appreciate modest, beneficial actions.

Celebrate small progress to create a happy and motivated culture.

Use of Descriptive Praise: Provide detailed praise to emphasize precisely what the youngster performed nicely.

For example, "I appreciate how you listened carefully and followed instructions."

Reward Systems: Implement a token economy where the youngster wins tokens or points for favorable conduct.

Exchange tokens for agreed-upon prizes, providing a real system of reinforcement.

Privilege System: Create a system where the youngster wins privileges for displaying excellent habits.

Privileges might include increased screen time, picking a family activity, or other favored activities.

Preferred Activities as Rewards: Allow the youngster to participate in chosen activities as a reward for completing assignments or demonstrating good behaviors.

Connect beneficial acts with joyful experiences.

Visual Reinforcement: Use charts or visual tools to demonstrate progress toward a goal.

Children can physically observe their successes, generating a feeling of accomplishment.

Consistent Positive Feedback: Provide continuous positive comments to support continuing efforts.

Consistency fosters a good atmosphere and emphasizes the importance of positive actions.

Point Systems: Assign points for completing tasks or displaying good actions.

Accumulated points might lead to awards or unique privileges.

Celebratory Rituals: Create small celebrating traditions for milestones, such as a special dinner or a family excursion.

The celebration underlines the value of excellent outcomes.

Contractual Agreements: Develop clear and straightforward contracts defining desired actions and related incentives.

Both parents and the kid may sign the contract, stressing commitment.

Team Approach: Involve the youngster in defining objectives and selecting incentives.

A collaborative approach empowers the youngster and improves their engagement in the reinforcing process.

Quality Time: Dedicate valuable time to spend with the youngster.

Positive attention and involvement build the parent-child relationship and act as a natural form of reinforcement.

Encouraging Independence: Reinforce and applaud efforts toward independence.

Encouraging independence improves self-esteem and a feeling of success.

Consistency, cheerfulness, and adaptability are crucial when employing positive reinforcement tactics. Tailor the methods to the child's preferences and be open to altering them depending on the child's answers and growth over time. Positive reinforcement not only helps regulate misbehavior but also enriches the parent-child bond.

Consistent Discipline Approaches

Consistency in punishment is key for properly regulating behaviors in children with attention deficit hyperactivity disorder (ADHD). Here are consistent disciplining techniques for parents:

Establish Clear Rules: Establish norms and expectations for conduct.

Ensure that regulations are basic, explicit, and age appropriate.

Consistent Consequences: Establish consistent consequences for both good and bad actions.

Consequences should be reasonable, fair, and directly tied to the conduct.

Positive Reinforcement: Reinforce favorable actions consistently with praise and prizes.

Acknowledge and praise desirable behaviors quickly to strengthen the link between good acts and favorable results.

Immediate Feedback: Provide instant feedback for both good and bad actions.

Immediate feedback helps the youngster grasp the implications of their behavior.

Predictable Routine: Implement a predictable daily routine.

Consistent routines help children with ADHD know what to anticipate, lowering anxiety and impulsivity.

Model Desired Behavior: Model the behaviors you wish to see in your kid.

Children generally learn by watching, so displaying desirable habits offers a good example.

Time-Outs: Use time-outs as a consistent penalty for unacceptable actions.

Ensure that time-outs are quick and unambiguous and offer the youngster a chance to reflect.

Privilege Removal: Remove privileges for a brief time if the youngster participates in unpleasant behaviors.

Linking consequences to actions boosts the efficacy of punishment.

Consistent Follow-Through: Follow through on established punishments regularly.

Inconsistency may confuse the youngster and decrease the effect of punishment.

Open Communication: Maintain open communication with the kid about expectations and consequences.

Ensure that the youngster knows the reasoning behind rules and punishments.

Problem-Solving Discussions: Engage in problem-solving talks with the youngster.

Encourage children to communicate their ideas and views, developing a sense of engagement and responsibility.

Logical Consequences: Apply logical consequences that are relevant to the conduct.

Logical consequences help the youngster comprehend the cause-and-effect link between acts and results.

Consistent Boundaries: Set consistent limits at home and outdoors.

Children benefit from clear and consistent expectations across multiple contexts.

Collaboration with School: Collaborate with teachers and school personnel to ensure consistency in rules and expectations.

A united strategy at home and school strengthens the child's grasp of behavioral rules.

Behavioral Charts: Use behavioral charts to convey expectations and progress.

Charts help youngsters monitor their behavior and comprehend the relationship between actions and outcomes.

Consistent discipline techniques contribute to a stable and supportive environment for children with ADHD. It helps kids grasp expectations, learn from their behaviors, and develop self-control. Regular communication and engagement with the kid, together with an emphasis on positive reinforcement, lead to a more effective and compassionate approach to punishment.

Behavioral Interventions in School

Implementing appropriate behavioral therapies in the school context is critical for treating adolescents with attention deficit hyperactivity disorder (ADHD). Here are some methods and interventions that instructors may apply to meet the special requirements of kids with ADHD:

Individualized Education Plan (IEP): Collaborate with parents, special education specialists, and other relevant stakeholders to construct an IEP for kids with ADHD.

Tailor academic objectives, accommodations, and behavioral methods to match the individual requirements of each kid.

Classroom Structure and Routine: Establish a controlled and predictable classroom atmosphere.

Clearly express daily routines and changes, offering visual timetables as required.

Visual Supports: Utilize visual aids such as charts, timetables, and reminders to promote organization and comprehension.

Visual aids help students follow instructions and manage their time successfully.

Clear and Concise Instructions: Provide clear and precise directions.

Break down activities into smaller pieces and repeat crucial material to guarantee comprehension.

Frequent Check-Ins: Implement frequent check-ins with the student to evaluate expectations and progress.

These quick conversations may give direction and encouragement for good actions.

Behavioral Contracts: Develop behavioral contracts detailing expectations, punishments, and incentives.

Involve the student in the development of the contract to foster a feeling of ownership.

Peer Support and Collaboration: Encourage peer support and cooperation.

Assign peer pals or companions to aid the kid with ADHD in remaining on target and comprehending instructions.

Flexible Seating Arrangements: Allow for flexible seating configurations to satisfy the demand for mobility.

Providing choices like fidget toys or standing workstations may help concentration and attention.

Modified Assignments: Modify assignments depending on the student's specific requirements and ability.

Break down jobs into digestible components and give further guidance as required.

Positive Reinforcement Systems: Implement a positive reinforcement system to recognize and reward desirable actions.

Regularly praise and acknowledge the learner for on-task conduct and successes.

Behavioral Interventions Team: Establish a behavioral intervention team to cooperate on specific student problems.

This team might comprise teachers, special education specialists, psychologists, and parents.

Social Skills Training: Incorporate social skills training within the curriculum.

Provide clear teaching and opportunity for kids with ADHD to practice and strengthen their social skills.

Regular Communication with Parents: Maintain open and frequent contact with parents.

Share ideas on the student's growth, discuss tactics that work effectively, and cooperate on consistent approaches at home and school.

Sensory Breaks: Allow for sensory breaks as required.

Designate a quiet and peaceful location where kids may take brief pauses to manage their sensory intake.

Professional Development for Educators: Provide continuing professional development for educators on ADHD awareness and effective methods.

Equip instructors with the knowledge and resources to build inclusive and supportive learning environments.

By integrating these behavioral treatments, educators may create an inclusive and supportive learning environment that meets the special needs of kids with ADHD. Regular communication with parents continued professional development, and tailored methods contribute to a complete and successful support system for kids with ADHD in the school context.

Individualized Education Program (IEP)

An Individualized Education Program (IEP) is a tailored plan developed to suit the educational requirements of individuals with disabilities. For kids with attention deficit hyperactivity disorder (ADHD), an IEP may play a critical role in providing individualized assistance and modifications. Here are the crucial components of an IEP for kids with ADHD:

Comprehensive Assessment: Conduct a comprehensive examination to discover the unique difficulties and capabilities of the student associated with ADHD.

Gather feedback from parents, teachers, and relevant professionals to guide the formulation of the IEP.

Clear and Measurable Goals: Establish specific and quantifiable academic and behavioral objectives for the kid.

Goals should be clear, realistic, and directly tied to alleviating the effect of ADHD on the student's learning.

Accommodations and Modifications: Outline adjustments and adaptations to accommodate the student's needs.

Examples include extra time on examinations, priority seating, modified assignments, and access to assistive technology.

Behavioral Strategies: Specify behavioral methods and treatments to address issues connected to ADHD.

This may involve the use of positive reinforcement, behavior contracts, and social skills training.

Individualized Instruction: Detail how education will be adjusted to the student's learning style and pace.

Consider customized education, small group activities, and extra assistance as required.

Collaboration with Specialized Professionals: Identify the participation of specialist experts, such as special education teachers, speech therapists, or occupational therapists.

Define their responsibilities in supporting the student's academic and behavioral requirements.

Regular Progress Monitoring: Establish a framework for continual progress monitoring.

Regularly review the student's performance and amend the IEP as required to ensure continuing improvement.

Transition Planning: Develop transition plans to prepare the student for changes in grade levels or transitions to post-secondary education and work.

Consider occupational training and life skills development as needed.

Parental Involvement: Encourage active parental engagement in the IEP process.

Seek comments from parents on the student's strengths, problems, and plans.

Social and Emotional Support: Include measures to treat the social and emotional elements of ADHD.

Consider the provision of counseling services or social skills training to assist the student's general well-being.

Regular IEP Meetings: Schedule frequent IEP meetings with teachers, parents, and related experts.

Use these sessions to monitor progress, address any obstacles, and amend the IEP as required.

Training for Educators: Provide training for educators and support workers on ADHD awareness and effective methods.

Ensure that all members of the educational team are well-informed on the student's requirements.

Transition Services for Post-Secondary Planning: Develop transition services that concentrate on preparing the kid for life after school.

Include conversations about job objectives, college plans, or vocational training.

Advocacy for the Student: Outline tactics for advocating for the student's needs within the school community.

This may involve boosting awareness among teachers and peers about ADHD-related issues.

Documentation and Review: Keep a careful record of the student's development and any revisions made to the IEP.

Conduct frequent evaluations to ensure the plan is successful and sensitive to the student's growing requirements.

By adopting a thorough and tailored IEP, educators and parents may cooperate to provide essential assistance for kids with ADHD. The plan should adapt over time depending on the student's success and changing requirements, promoting an inclusive and supportive educational environment.

Chapter 3: Medication Options

Overview of ADHD Medications

Medical therapy for attention deficit hyperactivity disorder (ADHD) generally includes the use of drugs to control symptoms. It's vital to emphasize that drug selections should be made in conjunction with healthcare specialists, considering the individual's particular requirements and circumstances. Here are some popular drug alternatives for ADHD:

Stimulant Medications: Methylphenidate: Available in many forms, including immediate-release and extended-release formulations. Common brand names include Ritalin, Concerta, and Metadate.

Amphetamine-based medications: Examples include Adderall, Dexedrine, and Vyvanse.

Stimulant medicines are considered the first-line therapy for ADHD. They operate by raising the amounts of neurotransmitters, such as dopamine and norepinephrine, in the brain, which helps increase attention and concentration.

Non-Stimulant Medications: Atomoxetine (Strattera): A non-stimulant drug that enhances norepinephrine levels. It is commonly used when stimulant drugs are not well-tolerated or if there are concerns about overuse.

Guanfacine (Intuniv) and Clonidine (Kapvay): These are alpha-2 adrenergic agonists that may aid with impulse control and hyperactivity.

Non-stimulant drugs are occasionally preferable for those who cannot tolerate stimulants or have comorbid illnesses that may contraindicate stimulant usage.

Lisdexamfetamine (Vyvanse): A long-acting stimulant that is metabolized to dextroamphetamine in the body. It delivers a steady delivery of drugs throughout the day.

Dexmethylphenidate (Focalin): A more concentrated version of methylphenidate is available in both immediate-release and extended-release forms.

Guanfacine ER (Intuniv) and Clonidine ER (Kapvay): Extended-release variants of guanfacine and clonidine, which are alpha-2 adrenergic agonists. They are taken once a day and may be used as alternatives to stimulant drugs.

Extended-Release Methylphenidate Formulations: Concerta, Metadate CD, Ritalin LA: Extended-release versions of methylphenidate, offering a longer duration of action compared to immediate-release forms.

Combination Medications: Amphetamine/Dextroamphetamine + Lisdexamfetamine: Some drugs combine multiple kinds of stimulants to give a more personalized approach to symptom management.

It's vital for anyone seeking medication for ADHD to speak with a healthcare practitioner, often a psychiatrist or a pediatrician with experience in ADHD. The choice of medicine relies on criteria such as the individual's age, medical history, the existence of comorbid diseases, and response to prior therapies.

Medication management for ADHD is frequently part of a complete treatment strategy that may also include behavioral treatments, educational initiatives, and support from parents, teachers, and mental health specialists. Regular monitoring and modifications to the treatment plan may be essential to enhance efficacy and reduce adverse effects.

Stimulant Medications

Stimulant drugs are often recommended for the treatment of attention deficit hyperactivity disorder (ADHD). These drugs operate by raising the amounts of neurotransmitters, such as dopamine and norepinephrine, in the brain, which helps enhance attention, concentration, and impulse control. Here are some regularly given stimulant drugs for ADHD:

Methylphenidate-based Medications:

Ritalin (Methylphenidate): Available in immediate-release and extended-release forms. Immediate-release forms may need to be taken numerous times a day, whereas extended-release forms give longer coverage.

Concerta (Methylphenidate ER): An extended-release formulation that gives a progressive release of medicine throughout the day.

Metadate CD (Methylphenidate ER): Another extended-release version of methylphenidate.

Daytrana (Methylphenidate transdermal system): A patch that distributes methylphenidate via the skin.

Amphetamine-based Medications:

Adderall (Mixed Amphetamine Salts): Contains a mixture of amphetamine salts. It is available in immediate-release and extended-release versions.

Dexedrine (Dextroamphetamine): Available in immediate-release and Spansule (extended-release) formulations.

Vyvanse (Lisdexamfetamine): A prodrug that is metabolized to dextroamphetamine in the body. It is a long-acting medicine.

Dexmethylphenidate (Focalin):

A more concentrated version of methylphenidate is available in immediate-release and extended-release forms.

It's crucial to note that individual reactions to stimulant drugs may vary, and the choice of prescription is typically dependent on criteria such as the patient's age, particular symptoms, and individual tolerance. The healthcare expert providing the drug will carefully analyze these criteria to develop the most effective treatment approach.

Stimulant drugs are typically deemed safe and effective when taken as recommended. However, like other drugs, they may have possible negative effects, and their usage should be supervised by a healthcare practitioner. Common adverse effects might include sleeplessness, lack of appetite, weight loss, and elevated heart rate. It's vital for patients using stimulant drugs to have frequent follow-up meetings with their healthcare practitioner to check the medication's efficacy and treat any possible adverse effects.

It's crucial to remember that the material presented here is for general informational purposes and should not substitute expert medical advice. Individuals seeking medication for ADHD should speak with a certified healthcare provider to evaluate their unique condition and choose the most effective course of therapy.

Non-Stimulant Medications

Non-stimulant drugs are commonly regarded as an option or supplement to stimulant medications for the treatment of attention deficit hyperactivity disorder (ADHD). These drugs act differently from stimulants, targeting various neurotransmitters in the brain. Here are some popular non-stimulant drugs used for ADHD:

Atomoxetine (Strattera): Atomoxetine is a selective norepinephrine reuptake inhibitor (NRI).

It boosts the amounts of norepinephrine in the brain, helping to enhance concentration and impulse control.

Atomoxetine is a non-stimulant choice that may be preferable for persons who cannot handle stimulant drugs or have a history of substance misuse.

Guanfacine (Intuniv): Guanfacine is an alpha-2 adrenergic agonist.

It impacts the prefrontal brain, helping to control attention, behavior, and working memory.

Guanfacine is widely used to control impulsivity, hyperactivity, and hostility associated with ADHD.

Clonidine (Kapvay): Clonidine, like guanfacine, is an alpha-2 adrenergic agonist.

It has a calming effect and may help lower hyperactivity, impulsivity, and hostility in persons with ADHD.

Clonidine may be used as an addition to stimulant drugs or as a main therapy.

These non-stimulant drugs are often explored when stimulant medications are not well-tolerated or are contraindicated. They may be especially beneficial for persons who have a history of drug misuse, tic disorders, or other problems that may be aggravated by stimulant usage.

It's crucial to remember that non-stimulant drugs may take longer to demonstrate therapeutic benefits compared to stimulants. It may take many weeks before the full advantages are noticed. As with any drug, there might be possible adverse effects, and consumers should work closely with their healthcare practitioner to monitor and change the treatment plan as required.

The decision between stimulant and non-stimulant drugs relies on numerous criteria, including the individual's unique symptoms, medical history, and reaction to prior therapies. Healthcare experts carefully analyze these criteria to design a tailored treatment plan that matches the specific requirements of each patient.

Consultation with Healthcare Professionals

Consulting with healthcare specialists is a vital step in the diagnosis and treatment of attention deficit hyperactivity disorder (ADHD). A multidisciplinary strategy combining several healthcare experts may assist in building a thorough and tailored treatment plan. Here are significant healthcare specialists engaged in the evaluation and treatment of ADHD:

Primary Care Physician (PCP): Many folks start by visiting their primary care provider.

The PCP may do an initial examination, obtain information regarding symptoms, and may refer to specialists for additional assessment.

Psychiatrist: Psychiatrists are medical practitioners who specialize in mental health.

They may give a more in-depth assessment, diagnose ADHD, and provide medication if considered necessary.

Psychologist: Psychologists are skilled in psychological examinations and treatments.

They may perform extensive tests to examine the cognitive and emotional components of ADHD and give treatment.

Neuropsychologist: Neuropsychologists specialize in studying the link between brain function and behavior.

They may do neuropsychological testing to examine cognitive processes and pinpoint particular areas of strength or struggle.

Pediatrician or Child Psychiatrist (for Children and Adolescents):

For children and adolescents, a pediatrician or child psychiatrist may be engaged in the evaluation and treatment of ADHD.

They may collaborate with parents, teachers, and other professionals to design an effective treatment plan.

Educational Specialist or School Psychologist: School-based experts may give useful insights into the academic and behavioral issues observed in the school context.

They may perform evaluations, interact with teachers, and aid in formulating educational plans, such as Individualized Education Programs (IEPs) or 504 plans.

Occupational Therapist: Occupational therapists can aid in resolving sensory and motor problems that may coexist with ADHD.

They may give ways to enhance organizational skills, motor coordination, and self-regulation.

Speech-Language Pathologist: Speech-language pathologists might be engaged if there are communication or language-related issues.

They may treat issues in expressive or receptive language abilities.

Counselor or Therapist: Counselors or therapists may offer emotional support and behavioral treatments for persons with ADHD and their families.

Behavioral therapy, cognitive-behavioral therapy, and family therapy are popular treatments.

Social Worker: Social workers may aid in addressing social and environmental problems impacting persons with ADHD.

They may give information, support services, and direction to families.

Adult ADHD Specialist: For adults with ADHD, contact with a healthcare practitioner specializing in adult ADHD is suggested.

Adult ADHD experts may include psychiatrists, psychologists, or other mental health practitioners.

Effective communication and cooperation among various healthcare providers, together with input from parents, teachers, and the person, contribute to a full picture of the individual's strengths, problems, and needs. The collaborative knowledge enables for the formulation of a well-rounded treatment plan that may include behavioral treatments, educational accommodations, and if required, pharmaceutical management. Regular follow-up and communication among team members are necessary for continuing evaluation and modifications to the treatment plan.

Benefits and Risks of Medication

Benefits of ADHD Medication:

Improved Focus and Attention: ADHD drugs, especially stimulants, may boost the capacity to concentrate and maintain attention.

Reduced Hyperactivity and Impulsivity: Medications assist in lowering hyperactivity and impulsive tendencies, enabling improved self-control.

Enhanced Executive Functioning: Medications may help executive functions such as planning, organizing, and time management.

Improved Academic and Occupational Performance: Many people see increases in academic or vocational performance with medication.

Increased Task Completion: Medications may lead to an enhanced capacity to finish activities and assignments.

Enhanced Social Interactions: Improved attention and less impulsivity may lead to more effective social interactions.

Positive Impact on Self-Esteem: Success in academic, professional, and social situations may favorably improve self-esteem and confidence.

Better Quality of Life: Effective medication management may lead to an overall higher quality of life for those with ADHD.

Risks and Considerations:

Side Effects: Common adverse effects of ADHD drugs may include sleeplessness, reduced appetite, weight loss, and elevated heart rate.

Individual Variability: Responses to drugs vary across people, and finding the proper medication and dose may need some trial and error.

Risk of Misuse: Stimulant drugs have a potential for overuse or abuse, even among those without ADHD.

Cardiovascular Risks: Stimulant drugs may have cardiovascular consequences, and persons with pre-existing cardiac issues should take them carefully.

Growth Suppression (in Children): Long-term use of stimulant drugs may be related to a modest slowdown of development in children, but this impact is normally minor.

Tolerance and Dependence: Some persons may acquire tolerance to the effects of stimulant medicines, and there is a possibility for dependency.

Individual Preferences: Not all persons with ADHD want to or need to take medication, and others may choose alternate ways.

Complexity of Treatment: Effective drug management frequently needs continual monitoring, modifications, and coordination with healthcare specialists.

It's crucial for persons contemplating medication for ADHD to participate in open discussions with healthcare experts, carefully analyze the possible advantages and hazards, and make educated choices based on their circumstances. Regular follow-up sessions are critical to assess the medication's efficacy, manage side effects, and make any required modifications to the treatment plan. Additionally, a complete therapy strategy may encompass behavioral therapies, psychoeducation, and support from healthcare practitioners, educators, and family members.

Monitoring and Adjusting Treatment Plans

Monitoring and changing treatment plans for attention deficit hyperactivity disorder (ADHD) is an important element of controlling the illness. This approach requires constant evaluation, feedback, and cooperation between the person, their caregivers, and healthcare experts. Here are crucial factors for evaluating and changing ADHD treatment plans:

Regular Follow-up Appointments: Schedule frequent follow-up visits with the healthcare expert overseeing the ADHD therapy.

Regular check-ins allow for continuing evaluation of the individual's reaction to the medicine, possible adverse effects, and overall improvement.

Symptom Monitoring: Keep a record of ADHD symptoms, including good developments and problems.

Tracking symptoms helps uncover trends and facilitates talks with healthcare practitioners.

Communication with Healthcare Professionals: Maintain open and honest contact with healthcare experts.

Report any changes in symptoms, side effects, or concerns quickly to permit rapid modifications to the treatment plan.

Feedback from Teachers and Caregivers: Gather comments from instructors, caretakers, and other persons engaged in the individual's everyday life.

Input from numerous sources offers a more thorough view of the individual's functioning.

Behavioral Interventions: Assess the efficacy of behavioral therapies alongside medicines.

Behavioral techniques may need to be altered depending on the individual's reaction and growing demands.

Educational Support: Collaborate with educators to monitor academic achievement and the efficacy of any educational adjustments.

Adjustments to educational plans, such as Individualized Education Programs (IEPs), may be essential.

Lifestyle Factors: Consider lifestyle variables that may affect ADHD symptoms, such as sleep, diet, and physical exercise.

Addressing these elements may contribute to overall well-being and treatment efficacy.

Individual Preferences: Take into consideration the individual's preferences and input about the treatment strategy.

Ensure that the therapy strategy matches the individual's objectives and values.

Medication Adjustments: If required, examine modifications to drug dose, schedule, or type.

Weight changes, growth trends (particularly in youngsters), and the development of tolerance may justify prescription modifications.

Reviewing Side Effects: Regularly evaluate possible adverse effects of medicine.

If side effects are harming the individual's well-being, suggest alternate drugs or changes to the present prescription.

Periodic Reassessment: Periodically evaluate the entire treatment strategy.

Consider if the existing strategy is satisfying the individual's requirements and whether revisions are required.

Transition Planning (for Adolescents and Adults): For teenagers advancing to maturity, and for adults, consider revisions to the treatment plan to address developing requirements.

Transition plans may incorporate conversations about education, jobs, and independent living.

Monitoring and changing treatment plans need a collaborative and proactive approach including the person, caregivers, educators, and healthcare experts. It's crucial to remember that treatment programs are dynamic and may require change over time to accommodate changing conditions and individual development. Regular evaluation ensures that the treatment plan stays connected with the individual's objectives and enhances their overall well-being.

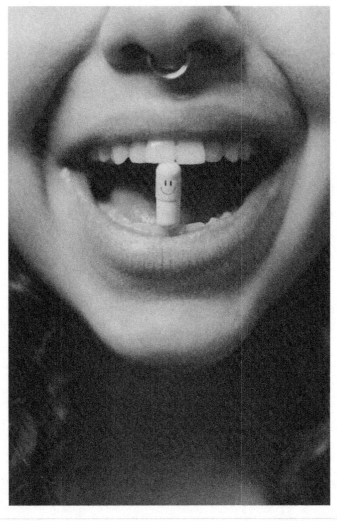

Chapter 4: Creating a Supportive Environment

Establishing Consistent Schedules

Establishing regular routines is critical for persons with attention deficit hyperactivity disorder (ADHD) to give structure, and predictability, and assist their daily functioning. Here are practical strategies for creating and keeping regular schedules:

Create a Visual Schedule: Use a graphic timetable that defines the daily routine.

Include visual clues, such as images or symbols, to make the timetable more accessible.

Set Regular Wake-up and Bedtime: Establish regular wake-up and bedtime habits.

Consistency in sleep rhythms adds to general well-being and helps manage mood and concentration.

Morning Routine: Develop a planned morning routine.

Include things like getting dressed, eating breakfast, and arranging items to start the day in a pleasant tone.

Allocate Specific Times for Activities: Assign precise times for various activities throughout the day.

These covers eating times, work or study hours, breaks, and leisure activities.

Use Timers or Alarms: Set alarms or timers to signify transitions between activities.

Auditory signals may help folks change attention and remain on course.

Consistent Mealtimes: Schedule regular and predictable mealtimes.

Maintaining a pattern for meals helps maintain energy levels and improves overall wellness.

Designated Work or Study Periods: Allocate dedicated periods for work, study, or concentrated activity.

Consistent intervals of concentrated labor may boost productivity.

Incorporate Breaks: Plan small pauses between jobs or activities.

Breaks allow for physical mobility and help reduce fatigue.

Organized Workspace: Create an orderly and clutter-free workstation.

A neat workplace aids in a focused and less distracting work or study setting.

Evening Routine: Establish a disciplined nightly routine.

Include things like slowing down, planning for the following day, and participating in relaxing hobbies.

Prioritize and Plan: Teach the significance of prioritizing tasks.

Help folks identify critical tasks and schedule their day appropriately.

Preparation for the Next Day: Encourage planning for the following day the night before.

This involves putting out clothing, arranging tools, and reviewing the timetable.

Limit Unnecessary Distractions: Identify and avoid unneeded distractions during planned activity.

Creating a concentrated workplace enhances attention and productivity.

Flexibility: Allow for some flexibility within the timetable.

Recognize that unexpected occurrences may occur, and people should be able to adjust without excessive stress.

Reflect and Adjust: Regularly examine the efficiency of the schedule.

Reflect on what worked well and what may be altered, and make improvements as required.

Consistent Bedtime: Maintain a regular bedtime, especially on weekends.

Consistent sleep habits lead to greater overall functioning.

Involve the Individual: Involve the person in planning and revising the timetable.

This develops a feeling of ownership and raises the chance of adherence.

Consistent schedules give a structure that helps persons with ADHD manage their time, decrease anxiety, and boost overall performance. By developing and sustaining routines, people may have enhanced predictability and a stronger sense of control over their daily activities.

Importance of Predictability

The value of regularity for persons with attention deficit hyperactivity disorder (ADHD) cannot be stressed. Predictability refers to the degree of certainty or consistency in the occurrence of events, routines, and expectations within an individual's environment. Establishing and sustaining regularity offers many major advantages for those with ADHD:

Reduced Anxiety and Stress: Predictability promotes a feeling of stability and eliminates ambiguity, which may considerably lessen anxiety levels in those with ADHD.

Knowing what to anticipate in particular scenarios may help decrease tension and encourage a more comfortable frame of mind.

Enhanced Time Management: Predictable routines aid people in managing their time properly.

Clear timetables and objectives make it simpler for persons with ADHD to organize and prioritize chores.

Improved Focus and Attention: Predictable surroundings give a structured framework that facilitates prolonged attention and concentration.

Consistent routines assist people in orienting their attention to the topic at hand without being continuously diverted by unanticipated changes.

Facilitates Planning and Organization: Predictability assists in the development of planning and organizing abilities.

Individuals with ADHD benefit from clear systems that help them to organize their ideas, actions, and activities more effectively.

Enhanced Self-Regulation: Predictable routines help to increase self-regulation.

Knowing what comes ahead assists people in preparing intellectually and emotionally for changes, lowering impulsive actions.

Increased Independence: Predictability supports independence by giving people a clear awareness of expectations and routines.

This lucidity helps them to negotiate everyday chores with more autonomy.

Consistent Sleep Patterns: Establishing a normal nighttime routine correlate to more consistent sleep habits.

Adequate and regular sleep favorably improves overall cognitive performance and emotional well-being.

Better Coping with Transitions: Predictability helps persons with ADHD manage more efficiently with changes between tasks.

Transitions are easier when people know what to anticipate, minimizing resistance or fear.

Supports Emotional Regulation: Predictable situations aid with emotional control.

Knowing the sequence of events and having clear expectations helps people control emotional reactions more efficiently.

Improved Academic Performance: Predictable routines and frameworks in educational environments favorably enhance academic achievement.

Clear expectations and predictable scheduling lead to higher engagement and learning results.

Enhanced Social Interactions: Predictability in social contexts helps persons with ADHD handle social interactions more readily.

Knowing the social expectations and procedures fosters healthy social interaction.

Increased Sense of Control: Predictability instills a feeling of control over one's surroundings and actions.

Individuals with ADHD frequently flourish when they feel they have a degree of control and agency in their everyday lives.

Creating predictability entails creating routines, setting clear expectations, and providing a structured atmosphere. This strategy meets the special requirements of persons with ADHD and adds to their general well-being and success in different facets of life.

Clear Communication and Expectations

Clear communication and well-defined expectations are key aspects in assisting persons with attention deficit hyperactivity disorder (ADHD). Establishing clarity in communication and expectations helps establish an organized and supportive atmosphere. Here are crucial tactics for good communication and creating expectations:

Use Simple and Direct Language: Communicate using basic and plain words.

Avoid unneeded complexity and offer facts to boost comprehension.

Use Visual Aids: Supplement verbal communication with visual tools.

Visual timetables, charts, or diagrams may aid those with ADHD in processing information more successfully.

Provide Clear Instructions: Break down instructions into simple and achievable stages.

Communicate what is required, and if necessary, repeat crucial facts to guarantee comprehension.

Establish Routines and Predictability: Communicate and develop patterns for everyday tasks.

Consistency and predictability assist persons with ADHD in anticipating and comprehending what will happen next.

Set Clear Expectations: Clarify expectations for behavior and duties.

Communicate the intended goals and the measures necessary to attain them.

Use Positive Framing: Frame instructions and expectations in a favorable way.

Emphasize what people should do rather than concentrating entirely on what they should avoid.

Provide Regular Feedback: Offer timely and precise comments on performance.

Positive reinforcement and constructive feedback assist people in realizing how effectively they are fulfilling expectations.

Establish Consequences: Clearly define the consequences for certain conduct.

Understanding the implications helps people make educated decisions.

Encourage Questions: Create an atmosphere where folks feel comfortable asking questions.

Encouraging explanation helps avoid misunderstandings.

Repeat and Reinforce: Repeat crucial information as required.

Reinforce essential expectations via repetition to promote recall.

Use Visual Cues for Transitions: Incorporate visual signals to convey changes between tasks.

Visual clocks or countdowns might help persons prepare for transitions.

Provide Advance Notice: Offer warning for changes in routines or planned activities.

This helps people to psychologically prepare for changes.

Clarify Priorities: Convey priorities and the significance of certain activities.

Help folks recognize which tasks are most vital and should be prioritized.

Involve Individuals in Goal setting: Involve people in creating their objectives.

This develops a feeling of ownership and responsibility for satisfying expectations.

Establish Clear Communication Channels: Ensure that communication routes are clear and accessible.

Establish regular mechanisms for folks to seek clarification or raise concerns.

Collaborate with Support Network: Collaborate with family members, educators, and healthcare providers to maintain constant communication.

A collaborative approach helps reinforce expectations across many situations.

Clear communication and establishing expectations assist not just those with ADHD but also others dealing with them. By establishing a common understanding and providing the appropriate support systems, persons with ADHD may navigate their everyday lives more efficiently and flourish in varied situations.

Breaking Down Tasks

Breaking down work into smaller, more manageable stages is a beneficial practice for those with attention deficit hyperactivity disorder (ADHD). This strategy helps reduce feelings of overload, boosts attention, and promotes effective work completion. Here's a tutorial on how to efficiently split down tasks:

Define the Task: Identify the work at hand.

Ensure a common understanding of what has to be completed.

Set Clear Objectives: Outline the objectives or aims of the assignment.

Clearly define what successful completion looks like.

Identify Key Components: Break the job into its major components or phases.

Identify the minor activities necessary to execute the larger job.

Sequence the Steps: Arrange the stages in a logical order.

Consider the sequence in which each step should be done.

Prioritize Steps: Determine the priority of each stage.

Identify which actions need to be accomplished first or take priority.

Use Visual Aids: Create visual aids, such as charts or diagrams, to depict the sequence of actions.

Visual clues may boost comprehension and memory.

Provide Examples:

Offer examples of how to complete each step.

Concrete examples help explain expectations.

Set Time Limits: Assign time limitations to each step.

Time limitations may help people remain focused and manage their time successfully.

Incorporate Breaks: Integrate small rests between stages.

Breaks help avoid mental tiredness and preserve continuous focus.

Monitor Progress: Establish a strategy to monitor progress.

Regularly check in on the fulfillment of stages.

Celebrate Milestones: Celebrate the accomplishment of each phase.

Acknowledge successes to offer positive reinforcement.

Provide Guidance: Offer advice and help as required.

Ensure that people feel comfortable seeking clarification or support.

Use Positive Reinforcement: Reinforce good actions and successful completion of stages.

Positive reinforcement boosts motivation and promotes continuing effort.

Adjust as Needed: Be flexible and open to alterations.

If stages prove problematic, adjust the method or give more help.

Encourage Self-Monitoring: Teach folks to monitor their growth.

Foster independence by developing self-awareness and self-assessment.

Seek Feedback: Encourage folks to share comments on the process.

Understand their experiences and make improvements based on their comments.

Review and Reflect: After finishing the work, evaluate the method.

Reflect on what worked well and explore adjustments for future projects.

Breaking down tasks is a talent that may be cultivated over time. It helps persons with ADHD to approach things in a methodical and orderly way, boosting the chance of success. By giving structure and clear expectations, breaking down work serves the special requirements of persons with ADHD and helps them handle their duties more efficiently.

Using Visual Aids

Using visual aids is a strong and successful method to treat persons with attention deficit hyperactivity disorder (ADHD). Visual aids give a clear and distinct manner to transmit information, increase learning, and promote organization. Here are numerous methods to employ visual assistance for those with ADHD:

Visual Schedules: Create graphic timetables that define daily habits and activities.

Use graphics, symbols, or icons to indicate distinct jobs and their order.

Develop checklists for chores and assignments.

Break down major projects into smaller, achievable segments, and utilize checkboxes for monitoring progress.

Charts & Graphs: Utilize charts and graphs to portray information graphically.

Visual representations may aid understanding, especially for numerical or sequential information.

Mind Maps: Use mind maps to graphically organize thoughts and ideas.

Mind maps may help people recognize links between ideas and prioritize information.

Color-Coding: Implement color-coding for distinct activities, topics, or priorities.

Color cues help humans swiftly recognize and organize information.

Visual Timers: Use visual clocks or countdowns to illustrate the passage of time.

Visual indicators for time management may aid with transitions between tasks.

Flowcharts: Create flowcharts to show processes or sequences of activities.

Flowcharts give a step-by-step visual roadmap for performing activities.

Flashcards: Use flashcards for learning and memorizing.

Include images together with crucial facts to boost remember.

Graphic Organizers: Implement graphic organizers for arranging and structuring thoughts.

Visual tools like Venn diagrams or idea maps may assist in organizing knowledge.

Visual Reminders: Place visual reminders in prominent settings.

Use sticky notes, posters, or pictures to remind folks about certain activities or habits.

Visual Cues for Transitions: Introduce visual signals to communicate changes between tasks.

Visual clues help humans anticipate changes in routine.

Token Systems: Implement token systems utilizing images to promote good actions.

Tokens or stickers serve as visible incentives for accomplishing tasks or displaying desirable behaviors.

Picture Exchange Communication System (PECS): For those with communication issues, try utilizing PECS.

PECS includes utilizing drawings to promote communication and communicate needs.

Visual Rules: Establish visual standards for certain surroundings or activities.

Clear and visible standards assist folks in comprehending expectations and behavioral norms.

Storyboarding: Use storyboarding to design and sequence tales or projects.

Storyboards graphically illustrate the sequence of events.

Visual Aids for Educational Concepts: Use graphics to teach abstract or complicated educational ideas.

Diagrams, charts, and pictures help make ideas more tangible.

Highlighting and Underlining: Encourage the usage of highlighting or emphasizing key information.

This visual contrast assists in concentrating attention on essential aspects.

When using visual aids, it's crucial to consider individual preferences and adjust the visuals to the unique requirements of the person with ADHD. Visual aids should be clear, concise, and connected to the information or job at hand. Regularly examine and update visual aids based on growing requirements and preferences. Overall, visual aids promote communication, organization, and comprehension, offering essential assistance for those with ADHD.

Chapter 5: Educational Support Collaboration with Teachers and School Staff

Collaboration with instructors and school personnel is vital for the achievement of kids with attention deficit hyperactivity disorder (ADHD). Working together ensures that the individual's specific demands are acknowledged and accommodated within the educational context. Here are essential methods for successful collaboration:

Open Communication: Establish open lines of communication between parents, teachers, and school personnel.

Regularly communicate information about the student's skills, problems, and development.

Share ADHD Accommodations: Communicate specific ADHD adjustments advised by healthcare specialists.

Ensure that teachers and school personnel are aware of and execute these modifications.

Develop an Individualized Education Program (IEP) or 504 Plan: Collaborate in the preparation of an Individualized Education Program (IEP) or a 504 Plan.

Identify adjustments, changes, and objectives to assist the student's academic performance.

Provide Teacher Training: Offer training workshops for teachers and school workers about ADHD.

Provide information on the features of ADHD, effective teaching practices, and how to build an ADHD-friendly classroom.

Regular Progress Meetings: Schedule monthly progress meetings with parents, teachers, and appropriate school officials.

Discuss the student's academic and behavioral progress, exchange thoughts, and alter techniques as appropriate.

Shared Goal setting: Collaboratively create academic and behavioral objectives for the student.

Ensure that objectives are reasonable, quantifiable, and connected with the student's particular requirements.

Establish a System for Communication and Feedback: Set up a framework for continual contact and feedback.

Utilize communication methods, such as emails, online platforms, or agendas, to keep everyone updated about the student's academic and social experiences.

Provide Resources and Materials: Share relevant information and materials with instructors.

Provide information on instructional practices, assistive technology, and therapies that may aid students with ADHD.

Encourage Differentiated Instruction: Encourage instructors to adopt differentiated education strategies.

Tailor teaching strategies to fit varied learning styles and meet individual requirements.

Address Behavioral Concerns Collaboratively: If behavioral problems occur, handle them together.

Work together to identify triggers, apply behavioral interventions, and reinforce good actions.

Utilize Support Staff: Collaborate with support personnel, such as special education teachers, counselors, and school psychologists.

Leverage the knowledge of these individuals to give extra help and resources.

Include the Student in Planning: Involve the student in planning and decision-making when appropriate.

Encourage self-advocacy and empower the learner to voice their needs.

Provide Professional Development Opportunities: Offer professional development opportunities on ADHD for all school personnel.

Enhancing the communal awareness of ADHD fosters a more inclusive and supportive educational climate.

Establish Consistent Classroom Routines: Work together to develop regular classroom procedures.

Predictable routines help kids with ADHD feel more confident and supported in the learning environment.

Celebrate Achievements: Celebrate academic and behavioral successes together.

Recognize and recognize progress, promoting a positive and collaborative attitude.

Effective cooperation between parents, teachers, and school personnel is vital for establishing an environment that promotes the academic, social, and emotional well-being of kids with ADHD. By promoting open communication, sharing resources, and working towards common objectives, the whole school community may contribute to the success of kids with ADHD.

Creating ADHD-Friendly Classrooms

Creating ADHD-friendly classrooms entails adopting techniques that cater to the special requirements of kids with attention deficit hyperactivity disorder (ADHD). These initiatives attempt to offer a helpful and inclusive learning environment. Here are crucial factors for developing ADHD-friendly classrooms:

Structured Environment: Establish a structured and orderly classroom atmosphere.

Delineate locations for various activities and keep regular procedures.

Visual Supports: Use visual assistance such as timetables, charts, and diagrams.

Visual tools give clear clues and help pupils comprehend expectations.

Seating Arrangements: Provide adaptable seating layouts.

Allow for choices like fidget toys, standing workstations, or alternate seating to meet varied learning styles and sensory demands.

Clear Instructions: Give clear and straightforward directions for jobs and assignments.

Break down instructions into smaller stages and verify for comprehension.

Visual Timers: Incorporate visible clocks or countdowns to manage time efficiently.

Visual cues assist kids with ADHD in better comprehending the notion of time and transitions.

Multisensory Learning: Incorporate multimodal learning activities.

Engage kids with ADHD via activities that incorporate sight, hearing, touch, and movement.

Consistent Routines: Establish regular daily habits.

Predictable routines make pupils feel safe and minimize worry.

Provide Clear Expectations: Clearly describe behavioral expectations.

Use visual reminders and positive reinforcement to promote desired actions.

Breaks and Movement: Allow for brief pauses and mobility throughout the classroom.

Incorporate physical exercises or brain breaks to help pupils release extra energy and enhance attention.

Use of Technology: Integrate technology to boost learning. Educational applications, interactive tools, and assistive technology help engage kids with ADHD.

Differentiated Instruction: Implement differentiated instruction methodologies.

Tailor teaching strategies to fit varied learning styles and meet individual requirements.

Flexible Grouping: Use flexible grouping for collaborative tasks.

Provide opportunities for both independent work and group engagement.

Minimize Distractions: Minimize unwanted distractions in the classroom.

Provide a quiet room for children who require it and utilize separators or headphones to limit noise.

Positive Reinforcement: Implement a positive reinforcement scheme.

Acknowledge and encourage good actions to inspire pupils.

Encourage Self-Advocacy: Foster self-advocacy skills in pupils.

Teach kids to express their needs and preferences to both instructors and peers.

Support from Peers: Encourage peer support and understanding.

Foster a classroom atmosphere where students support and appreciate one another's diversity.

Collaboration with Parents: Maintain open contact with parents.

Share ideas regarding the student's development, obstacles, and techniques that work effectively in the classroom.

Professional Development: Provide professional development opportunities for instructors on ADHD.

Enhance the communal awareness of ADHD to build a more inclusive atmosphere.

Regular Check-Ins: Conduct frequent check-ins with pupils.

Ask for feedback and change techniques depending on the requirements of each learner.

By providing ADHD-friendly classrooms, educators contribute to a pleasant and supportive learning environment where children with ADHD may succeed academically, socially, and emotionally. Implementing these tactics creates inclusion and meets the specific requirements of each kid with ADHD.

Adaptive Teaching Strategies

Adaptive teaching practices are vital for educators to address the different learning demands of children, especially those with attention deficit hyperactivity disorder (ADHD). These tactics seek to promote an inclusive and supportive learning environment. Here are adaptive teaching practices that might assist kids with ADHD:

Differentiated Instruction: Tailor training to meet varied learning styles and abilities.

Offer different opportunities for students to obtain and show comprehension of material.

Flexible Seating: Provide seating alternatives that cater to diverse sensory demands.

Allow for alternate sitting configurations, such as standing workstations, fidget gadgets, or pillows.

Clear and Concise Instructions: Deliver unambiguous directions.

Break down complicated activities into simple parts and give visual hints.

Use of Visual Aids: Incorporate visual aids, charts, and diagrams.

Visual aids boost knowledge and help with organizing.

Structured Routines: Establish regular and regulated daily habits.

Clearly express transitions and modifications in the timetable.

Multisensory Learning: Engage students with ADHD with multimodal learning activities.

Include hands-on activities, movement, and interactive aspects.

Visual Timers and Countdowns: Integrate graphic clocks and countdowns for time management.

Visual clues help pupils comprehend the notion of time and prepare for changes.

Breaks and Movement Opportunities: Allow for brief rests and mobility chances.

Incorporate physical exercises or mental breaks to help pupils release energy and retain attention.

Interactive Technology: Utilize interactive technologies to boost engagement.

Educational applications, interactive whiteboards, and digital technologies may promote learning.

Chunking Information: Break down knowledge into smaller, manageable parts.

Present material in a systematic and ordered way.

Flexible Grouping: Use flexible grouping tactics for collaborative tasks.

Provide opportunities for both independent work and group engagement.

Provide Choices: Offer alternatives in tasks and projects.

Allowing pupils considerable liberty develops a feeling of control and participation.

Positive Reinforcement: Implement a positive reinforcement scheme.

Acknowledge and reward good behaviors to inspire and reinforce desirable activities.

Encourage Self-Monitoring: Teach self-monitoring skills.

Help children with ADHD become aware of their strengths and problems and learn to manage their behavior.

Regular Check-Ins: Conduct frequent check-ins with pupils.

Provide an opportunity for kids to voice concerns, share progress, and address any issues they may be having.

Utilize Support Staff: Collaborate with support personnel, such as special education teachers and counselors.

Leverage the experience of specialist individuals to give extra help.

Encourage Peer Support: Foster a supportive classroom atmosphere.

Encourage peer support and understanding, creating an atmosphere where students assist one another.

Promote Organizational Skills: Teach and reinforce organizing skills.

Provide tools, such as planners or checklists, to enable students to manage their assignments and obligations.

Flexibility and Patience: Demonstrate flexibility and patience.

Understand that kids with ADHD may need more time or help and be patient with their distinct learning experiences.

Adaptive teaching practices identify the requirements of kids with ADHD and offer an inclusive learning environment that encourages achievement and well-being. By adopting these tactics, educators may support the different learning styles and talents of all children in their classes.

Special Education Services

Special education services serve a critical role in providing individualized assistance for kids with attention deficit hyperactivity disorder (ADHD) and other learning challenges. These programs are meant to meet particular needs and guarantee that students get an education that suits their unique circumstances. Here are the major components of special education programs for kids with ADHD:

Individualized Education Program (IEP): Develop an Individualized Education Program (IEP) for kids with ADHD.

The IEP contains precise objectives, adjustments, modifications, and support services customized to the student's requirements.

504 Plan: Consider a 504 Plan for kids with ADHD who may not need special education but need accommodations.

A 504 Plan makes specific adjustments or changes to enable children to engage fully in the general education environment.

Specialized Instruction: Provide specific training to overcome academic issues linked with ADHD.

Individual or small-group training may be essential to promote learning in certain subject areas.

Behavioral Interventions: Implement behavioral therapies to address difficulties linked to attention, impulsivity, and hyperactivity.

Positive behavior support measures may be integrated into the student's plan.

Resource Room Support: Offer resource room help for further aid with academic activities.

A resource room may offer a calmer and more organized setting for study.

Speech and Language Therapy: Provide speech and language therapy if language-related problems are apparent.

Speech therapy may treat communication issues and enhance language abilities.

Occupational Therapy: Offer occupational therapy to address sensory and motor problems.

Occupational therapists may give ways to enhance fine and gross motor abilities.

Counseling Services: Provide counseling services to address social and emotional well-being.

Individual or group therapy may benefit kids in building coping skills and controlling emotions.

Assistive Technology: Integrate assistive technology to help academic pursuits.

Tools such as text-to-speech software or graphic organizers may boost accessibility.

Extended Time on Assessments: Allow for longer time on evaluations and testing.

Additional time accommodates processing problems linked with ADHD.

Flexible Grading: Implement flexible grading methods.

Consider alternate evaluation approaches that rely on comprehension rather than speed.

Behavioral Contracts: Develop behavioral contracts defining expectations and penalties.

Behavioral contracts may be a collaborative method of engaging children, parents, and instructors to encourage beneficial behaviors.

Collaboration with Regular Education Teachers: Facilitate cooperation between special education instructors and normal education teachers.

Regular communication ensures that accommodations and changes are regularly applied.

Transition Planning: Develop transition strategies for kids transitioning between grade levels or educational settings.

Transition planning helps children manage transitions easily.

Parental Involvement: Encourage parental engagement in the formulation and evaluation of the student's IEP or 504 Plan.

Collaborate with parents to ensure a comprehensive grasp of the student's requirements.

Training for School Staff: Provide training for school workers on ADHD awareness and effective interventions. Increased understanding strengthens the capacity of instructors to help pupils with ADHD.

Regular Progress Monitoring: Implement frequent progress monitoring.

Assess the efficacy of treatments and make modifications depending on the student's development.

Positive Reinforcement Programs: Establish positive reinforcement programs.

Reinforce desirable behaviors with a system of incentives and recognition.

Social Skills Training: Integrate social skills training into the curriculum.

Social skills programs may benefit students in establishing successful interpersonal skills.

Special education programs attempt to establish a supportive and inclusive educational environment that helps kids with ADHD to attain their full potential. The cooperation between educators, support workers, parents, and students is vital in ensuring that these programs properly meet the specific requirements of each person.

Accommodations and Modifications

Accommodations and modifications are crucial components of providing successful assistance for kids with attention deficit hyperactivity disorder (ADHD) in an educational context. These adaptations are aimed to guarantee that kids with ADHD have equal access to school and can participate in the learning process. Here's a breakdown of accommodations and modifications:

Accommodations:

Extended Time: Allow more time for completing assignments, examinations, and exams.

Additional time addresses possible issues with time management.

Frequent Breaks: Provide opportunities for brief pauses throughout work or activities.

Breaks may assist kids with ADHD in controlling restlessness and retaining attention.

Preferential Seating: Seat the learner at a spot that limits distractions and allows for better focus.

Consider closeness to the instructor or away from unwanted distractions.

Visual Supports: Use visual aids, charts, or graphic organizers to support spoken directions.

Visual aids may boost knowledge and organizing.

Assistive Technology: Integrate assistive technology aids, such as speech-to-text software or electronic organizers.

Technology can benefit pupils in numerous academic pursuits.

Alternative Assignments: Offer alternate tasks or projects that appeal to individual talents and interests.

Providing alternatives boosts engagement and motivation.

Flexible Grading: Implement flexible grading techniques.

Emphasize knowledge and effort above speed or finish time.

Use of Fidget Tools: Allow the use of fidget gadgets or sensory aides discreetly.

These methods may help reduce restlessness and enhance attention.

Quiet Work Environment: Provide a quiet work environment or a defined location with minimal stimulation.

A tranquil atmosphere enhances attention and minimizes distractions.

Break Tasks into Smaller Steps: Break down complicated activities into smaller, more doable stages.

This technique helps students approach tasks systematically.

Modifications:

Altered Assignments: Modify assignments to match the student's ability and customized objectives.

Adjusting the degree of difficulty may promote effective completion.

Simplified Instructions: Simplify and clarify instructions for assignments and activities.

Use plain language to promote comprehension.

Reduced Workload: Reduce the amount of work necessary for assignments or homework.

Focus on important principles to avoid overloading the learner.

Alternative Assessments: Offer alternate tests that measure the student's comprehension in multiple ways.

Options may include projects, presentations, or practical demonstrations.

Modified Grading Criteria: Adjust grading standards to reflect the specific development of the learner.

Emphasize development and progress above satisfying old criteria.

Peer Assistance: Facilitate peer help or mentorship.

Pairing kids with a peer buddy for tasks foster teamwork and support.

Customized Learning Materials: Provide customized learning materials, including modified texts or resources.

Tailored materials may make information more accessible.

Individualized Homework Plans: Develop tailored assignment programs depending on the student's requirements.

Set reasonable expectations and prioritize vital activities.

Specialized Instruction: Offer customized teaching in certain areas or skills.

Addressing areas of difficulty directly may promote academic progress.

Individualized Testing Formats: Modify testing methods, such as offering oral examinations or permitting responses in numerous forms.

This enables varied learning and expressive styles.

It's vital to individualize adjustments and modifications depending on the specific requirements of each kid with ADHD.

Regular communication between instructors, parents, and the student ensures that the assistance offered is effective and sensitive to the student's growing requirements. Additionally, frequent assessments and revisions to accommodation plans are important to reflect any changes in the student's academic needs.

Chapter 6: Lifestyle Factors

Incorporating Physical Activity

Incorporating physical exercise is a good method for those with attention deficit hyperactivity disorder (ADHD). Regular exercise has been found to favorably influence attention, executive function, and general well-being. Here are strategies to include physical exercise in everyday living for those with ADHD:

Structured Physical Activities: Engage in organized physical activities such as team sports, swimming, martial arts, or dancing lessons.

Participating in organized activities gives a schedule and social connection.

Outdoor Play: Encourage outside play and discovery.

Activities like riding, hiking, or playing in a park give chances for exercise and fresh air.

Daily Walks: Incorporate regular walks within the program.

Walking may be a simple but effective technique to encourage physical exercise and enhance attention.

Active Commuting: Consider active commuting choices, such as walking or bicycling to school or work.

Active transportation adds physical exercise to regular activities.

Yoga or Tai Chi: Explore hobbies like yoga or tai chi, which concentrate on mindfulness and physical movement.

These routines may assist in enhancing attention and decrease stress.

Playground Exercises: Use playground equipment for workouts.

Activities like climbing, swinging, and leaping add to general physical fitness.

Dance and Movement: Encourage dancing or movement-based activities.

Dancing to music or participating in rhythmic motions may be fun and useful.

Home Exercise Routines: Establish home exercise regimens.

Simple workouts or activities like jumping jacks, stretching, or yoga may be done at home.

Gardening: Involve folks in gardening activities. Gardening gives a hands-on and interesting method to be physically active.

Active Games: Play energetic games that include mobility. Games like tag, hide-and-seek, or sports-related video games may be entertaining and active.

Fitness Challenges: Create fitness challenges or objectives. Setting reasonable physical activity goals and evaluating success may be motivating.

Joining Clubs or Teams: Consider joining groups or teams that concentrate on physical activity. Being part of a group promotes social contact and a feeling of community.

Adaptive Sports: Explore adapted sports or activities customized to individual tastes and abilities. Adaptive sports programs may provide adjusted activities for diverse requirements.

Mindful Movement Practices: Introduce mindful movement methods like qigong or mindful walking.

Combining exercise with mindfulness practices helps boost attention and awareness.

Physical Education Classes: Enroll in physical education courses that fit with personal interests.

Pursuing activities, one likes makes it more likely to remain active.

It's crucial to adjust physical activity to individual interests and abilities. Regular physical exercise not only adds to physical health but also enhances cognitive function and emotional well-being, making it a key component of ADHD care. Always speak with healthcare providers before beginning any new fitness plan, particularly for persons with underlying health problems

Benefits of Exercise for ADHD

Exercise has several advantages for those with attention deficit hyperactivity disorder (ADHD), addressing both physical and cognitive elements. Here are numerous benefits of adding regular exercise into the routine of those with ADHD:

Improved Focus and Attention: Exercise has been demonstrated to boost cognitive abilities, particularly attention and concentration.

Physical exercise stimulates the production of neurotransmitters including dopamine and norepinephrine, which play a critical role in attention management.

Enhanced Executive Function: Regular exercise improves the growth and enhancement of executive functions such as planning, organization, and impulse control.

These cognitive abilities are typically areas of struggle for persons with ADHD.

Regulation of Neurotransmitters: Exercise helps control neurotransmitters related to ADHD, such as dopamine and serotonin.

Balancing these neurotransmitters may significantly improve mood, motivation, and general well-being.

Reduced Hyperactivity and Impulsivity: Physical activity gives an outlet for surplus energy, helping to lessen hyperactivity.

Exercise may also help to greater impulse control.

Enhanced Mood and Stress Reduction: Exercise provides mood-boosting benefits by increasing the synthesis of endorphins, the body's natural feel-good compounds.

Regular physical exercise may help decrease stress and anxiety, which are typically connected with ADHD.

Improved Sleep Quality: Engaging in regular exercise may lead to better sleep quality.

Quality sleep is vital for those with ADHD, as it enhances general well-being and cognitive performance.

Increased Brain-Derived Neurotrophic Factor (BDNF): Exercise has been related to higher levels of Brain-Derived Neurotrophic Factor (BDNF), a protein that promotes the development and maintenance of neurons.

Higher levels of BDNF are related to enhanced cognitive performance.

Enhanced Academic Performance: Regular physical exercise has been connected with greater academic achievement.

Improved concentration and cognitive function coming from exercise may significantly improve learning and academic results.

Social Engagement: Participating in group activities or team sports improves social contact.

Social interaction may lead to enhanced self-esteem and a feeling of belonging.

Establishment of Routine: Incorporating exercise into a regular program gives structure and consistency.

A well-established routine may help persons with ADHD manage their time and duties more successfully.

Improved Self-Esteem: Achieving physical fitness objectives via exercise may enhance self-esteem and confidence.

A good self-image is vital for those with ADHD, who may confront difficulty in different areas.

Stress Relief and Emotional Regulation: Physical exercise works as a natural stress reliever.

Engaging in exercise gives an avenue for emotional expression and may help with emotional management.

Development of Healthy Habits: Encouraging frequent exercise supports the building of good living patterns.

Consistent physical exercise adds to general health and well-being.

It's crucial to remember that the advantages of exercise might differ across people, and the kind and intensity of exercise should be adapted to specific preferences and abilities. Before beginning any new workout regimen, particularly for persons with underlying health concerns, it's essential to contact healthcare specialists.

Finding Suitable Activities

Finding acceptable activities for persons with attention deficit hyperactivity disorder (ADHD) includes examining their interests, preferences, and skills. It's crucial to find activities that correspond with their requirements and create a good and engaging experience. Here are some recommendations for choosing appropriate activities:

Explore Interests: Identify the individual's interests and hobbies.

Activities relating to personal interests are more likely to be pleasurable and engaging.

Consider Preferences: Take into consideration the individual's preferences for activities.

Some folks may like outdoor hobbies, while others may appreciate creative or inside endeavors.

Trial and Error: Experiment with various activities to see what works best.

Be open to exploring many possibilities to identify activities that captivate the individual's interest.

Incorporate Variety: Introduce a range of activities to avoid boredom.

A blend of physical, artistic, and cognitive activities may accommodate diverse tastes.

Adjust Intensity Levels: Consider the individual's energy levels and attention span.

Adjust the intensity and length of exercises to meet their capacities.

Social or Solo Activities: Determine if the person enjoys sociable or independent activities.

Some may flourish in communal situations, while others may prefer more solitary hobbies.

Adapt Activities: Adapt activities to fit individual requirements.

Modify regulations or characteristics of the activity to make it more accessible and pleasant.

Structured vs. Unstructured Activities: Evaluate preferences for organized versus unstructured activities.

Some people may flourish in controlled situations, while others may prefer more freedom.

Consider Sensory Preferences: Consider sensory preferences.

Some people may like activities that give sensory input, while others may be sensitive to specific stimuli.

Encourage Hobbies: Encourage the growth of hobbies.

Hobbies give a consistent and meaningful method to connect with activities throughout time.

Set Realistic Goals: Establish reasonable objectives for activities.

Break things into small chunks and celebrate triumphs, encouraging a feeling of completion.

Involve Others: Involve family members, friends, or classmates in activities.

Social interaction may increase the pleasure of activities and give extra assistance.

Mindfulness and Relaxation Activities: Explore mindfulness or relaxation practices.

Techniques such as yoga or meditation may aid with concentration and stress reduction.

Outdoor and Nature Activities: Consider outdoor activities and contact with nature.

Outdoor surroundings may offer a dynamic and peaceful background for activities.

Educational Games and Puzzles: Explore educational games, puzzles, or brain teasers.

Activities that challenge the intellect may be both pleasurable and healthy.

Team Sports or Individual Pursuits: Assess preferences for team sports versus independent interests.

Both alternatives provide distinct advantages, and the individual's temperament may determine the decision.

Creative Outlets: Encourage creative outlets such as sketching, painting, or music.

Creative activities give an expressive and engaging form of participation.

Regularly Assess Preferences: Regularly examine and update the list of favored activities.

Interests and preferences may develop, and changing activities appropriately promotes continuing involvement.

Tailoring activities to individual tastes and requirements is vital for generating a good and gratifying experience for those with ADHD. Regular communication and feedback may assist in modifying activity selections depending on the individual's growing interests and preferences.

Promoting Healthy Eating Habits

Nutritional Considerations

Nutritional considerations for persons with attention deficit hyperactivity disorder (ADHD) are vital to maintain general well-being and manage any issues connected with the illness. Here are special dietary concerns for persons with ADHD:

Omega-3 Fatty Acids: Include sources of omega-3 fatty acids in the diet, such as fatty fish (e.g., salmon, mackerel), flaxseeds, chia seeds, and walnuts.

Omega-3 fatty acids have been examined for their possible cognitive and emotional advantages.

Protein-Rich Foods: Ensure an appropriate diet of protein from sources such as lean meats, poultry, fish, eggs, dairy products, legumes, and plant-based proteins.

Protein stimulates the generation of neurotransmitters linked with concentration and attention.

Complex Carbohydrates: Choose complex carbs such as whole grains, fruits, and vegetables.

These carbs give a continuous flow of energy, ensuring stable blood sugar levels.

Balanced Meals: Encourage balanced meals that contain a variety of carbs, proteins, and healthy fats.

Balanced meals lead to maintained energy levels and enhanced attention.

Vitamins and Minerals: Ensure an appropriate intake of important vitamins and minerals, including vitamin D, B vitamins, iron, zinc, and magnesium.

These nutrients have functions in cognitive function and general wellness.

Limit Sugars and Processed Foods: Reduce the intake of sugary meals and drinks, as well as processed and refined foods.

These may lead to energy oscillations and may influence attention and behavior.

Hydration: Promote consistent hydration with water throughout the day.

Dehydration may influence cognitive performance and maintaining well-hydrated benefits general health.

Avoid Artificial Additives: Limit the consumption of artificial additives, colorings, and preservatives in food.

Some persons with ADHD may be sensitive to substances.

Consider Elimination Diets: In conjunction with healthcare specialists, try elimination diets to detect and manage any food sensitivities.

Certain people may benefit from avoiding particular allergies or trigger foods.

Regular Meals and Snacks: Encourage frequent meals and snacks scattered throughout the day.

Consistent eating routines may help normalize blood sugar levels.

Limit Caffeine and Stimulants: Monitor and restrict the consumption of coffee and stimulants.

Excessive coffee consumption might interfere with sleep and increase symptoms of ADHD.

Individualized Nutrition Plans: Work with healthcare specialists, particularly dietitians or nutritionists, to design tailored dietary regimens.

Tailor dietary counsel based on the individual's personal requirements, preferences, and any existing health issues.

Mealtime Structure: Establish established mealtime patterns.

Predictable routines may assist persons with ADHD in managing their time and minimizing impulsivity during meals.

Supportive Family Environment: Foster a supportive family atmosphere that supports healthy eating habits.

Engage family members in choosing healthful food choices and establishing a happy mealtime setting.

Monitor Nutrient Intake: Monitor nutrient intake to verify that the person is reaching their nutritional requirements.

Adjust the diet as required to correct any deficiencies or imbalances.

It's crucial to remember that individual reactions to dietary changes may differ. Consulting with healthcare specialists, especially a licensed dietitian or nutritionist, is vital for designing tailored and successful dietary recommendations for persons with ADHD. Additionally, any large dietary modifications should be made gradually, and continual monitoring of nutritional status is important.

Potential Impact of Diet on ADHD Symptoms

The possible influence of nutrition on attention deficit hyperactivity disorder (ADHD) symptoms is a subject of continuing study and debate.

While the association between nutrition and ADHD is complicated and varies across people, several dietary components may impact symptoms. It's crucial to emphasize that nutritional changes should be addressed carefully, and individual responses might vary. Here are some thoughts addressing the possible influence of nutrition on ADHD symptoms:

Omega-3 Fatty Acids: Some studies show that omega-3 fatty acids, present in fatty fish, flaxseeds, and walnuts, may have potential advantages for cognitive function and attention.

Omega-3 supplementation has been examined as a supplemental remedy, but further study is required to confirm its usefulness.

Protein and Amino Acids: Protein-rich diets provide amino acids that are precursors of neurotransmitters, such as dopamine and norepinephrine, which are important in attention and concentration.

A balanced intake of proteins may boost the generation of these neurotransmitters.

Sugar with Artificial Additives: While there is no definitive evidence connecting sugar to ADHD, certain people may be vulnerable to the effects of excessive sugar consumption.

Some research reveals a possible relationship between artificial food colorings and preservatives and increased hyperactivity in some youngsters. However, the data is not consistent, and additional study is required.

Elimination Diets: Elimination diets, which entail eliminating certain foods or dietary groupings to uncover possible triggers, have been examined.

Some people may exhibit improvements in ADHD symptoms after removing allergies or trigger foods. However, the effectiveness of elimination diets is not generally acknowledged, and they should be undertaken under the advice of healthcare specialists.

Iron and Zinc: Adequate amounts of iron and zinc are needed for cognitive function, and deficits in these minerals may influence attention and concentration.

Ensuring a balanced diet with appropriate iron and zinc is vital for general health.

Caffeine: Caffeine, present in coffee, tea, and certain soft drinks, is a stimulant that may have varied effects on persons with ADHD.

While some find that coffee increases concentration, excessive consumption may lead to jitteriness and interrupt sleep.

Individual Responses: Individual reactions to nutrition may vary greatly, and what works for one person may not be beneficial for another.

Keeping a food diary and tracking changes in behavior or symptoms might help discover possible dietary factors.

It's crucial to address dietary therapies for ADHD in a tailored way and under the advice of healthcare specialists. Before making substantial modifications to a diet, consultation with a licensed dietitian, nutritionist, or healthcare practitioner is suggested. Additionally, comprehensive ADHD care often entails a mix of behavioral interventions, educational assistance, and, in some situations, medication.

Chapter 7: Sleep and Relaxation

Establishing a Healthy Sleep Routine

Establishing a regular sleep schedule, often known as excellent sleep hygiene, is critical for those with attention deficit hyperactivity disorder (ADHD). A regular and tranquil nighttime ritual may help control sleep patterns and enhance overall sleep quality. Here's a guide on maintaining a good sleep regimen for those with ADHD:

Set a Consistent Sleep Schedule: Establish a consistent sleep routine by going to bed and getting up at the same time every day, including weekends.

Consistency helps regulate the body's internal clock.

Create a Relaxing Bedtime Routine: Develop a relaxing ritual leading up to sleep.

Activities may include reading a book, having a warm bath, practicing relaxation techniques, or participating in mild stretching.

Limit Screen Time Before Bed: Reduce exposure to devices (phones, tablets, laptops) at least an hour before sleep.

The blue light released by screens may impair the generation of melatonin, a hormone that governs sleep.

Prepare the Sleep Environment: Make the bedroom favorable to sleep by keeping it cold, dark, and quiet.

Consider utilizing blackout curtains, white noise machines, or earplugs if required.

Choose Comfortable Bedding: Ensure that the bed and sheets are comfy.

Invest in a quality mattress and pillows to boost sleep comfort.

Limit Stimulants in the Evening: Avoid stimulants such as coffee and nicotine in the hours preceding up to sleep.

These drugs may interfere with the ability to fall asleep.

Encourage Wind-Down Activities: Engage in calming activities in the hour before sleep.

Activities could include listening to relaxing music, doing deep breathing techniques, or indulging in mild stretching.

Create a Sleep-Inducing Atmosphere: Dim the lights in the evening to indicate to the body that it's time to wind down.

Consider utilizing soft, warm lighting to create a friendly ambiance.

Avoid Heavy Meals Before Bed: Avoid big or heavy meals close before sleep.

If hungry, go for a small snack that won't interrupt sleep.

Establish a Routine for Children: If the client is a youngster, develop a regular nighttime routine that includes activities like brushing teeth, reading a tale, or listening to relaxing music.

Monitor Sleep Patterns: Keep note of sleep patterns and change the regimen as required.

Regular monitoring may assist in discovering variables that may be impacting sleep.

Encourage Daytime Sun Exposure: Encourage exposure to natural sunshine throughout the day.

Natural light helps regulate the body's internal clock and promotes the sleep-wake cycle.

Regular Exercise: Encourage frequent physical exercise throughout the day.

However, avoid strenuous exertion close to sleep.

Limit Naps: If sleeping is unavoidable, restrict it to a short period (20-30 minutes) and avoid napping late in the day.

Consult with Healthcare Professionals: If sleep troubles continue, speak with healthcare specialists, such as a sleep specialist or healthcare provider.

They may assist in discovering underlying difficulties and give recommendations on increasing sleep.

By combining these behaviors into a daily routine, persons with ADHD may establish a supportive environment for peaceful and regular sleep. It's vital to personalize the routine to individual tastes and requirements, and modifications may be required depending on continued monitoring of sleep patterns.

Importance of Consistent Bedtimes

Consistent bedtimes serve a critical role in ensuring excellent sleep hygiene and general well-being, especially for persons with attention deficit hyperactivity disorder (ADHD). Here are some significant reasons stressing the need for regular bedtimes:

Regulates Circadian Rhythms: Consistent bedtimes assist in controlling the body's circadian rhythms, which are inherent biological activities that follow a roughly 24-hour pattern.

Maintaining a consistent sleep pattern strengthens the body's internal clock, supporting a predictable sleep-wake cycle.

Optimizes Sleep Quality: A constant bedtime provides patients adequate time to complete the whole sleep cycle, including key phases like deep sleep and REM (rapid eye movement) sleep.

Quality sleep helps physical and mental well-being, including better cognitive performance and mood management.

Enhances Sleep Onset: Regular bedtimes may increase the capacity to fall asleep easily.

Predictable sleep habits indicate to the body that it's time to wind down, making it simpler to transition into sleep.

Improves Sleep Efficiency: Consistent bedtimes promote sleep efficiency, which refers to the amount of time spent sleeping relative to the overall time spent in bed.

Efficient sleep habits help to feel refreshed upon awakening.

Supports Cognitive Function: Well-regulated sleep patterns significantly enhance cognitive function, including attention, memory, and decision-making.

Individuals with ADHD may see improvements in attention and executive function with regular and adequate sleep.

Reduces Sleep Disruptions: A consistent sleep routine helps reduce disturbances throughout the night.

Individuals with ADHD may be more prone to sleep problems, making it vital to create a regular nighttime regimen.

Promotes Emotional Well-Being: Adequate and regular sleep is connected to emotional well-being and mood stability.

Establishing a dependable sleep routine might help to a more happy and emotionally balanced attitude.

Manages ADHD Symptoms: Consistent sleep patterns may have a role in treating ADHD symptoms, including hyperactivity, impulsivity, and inattention.

Quality sleep promotes overall ADHD management efforts.

Facilitates Daily Routine: A regular bedtime helps build a planned daily habit.

Individuals with ADHD benefit from consistent routines, as they create a feeling of order and help manage time efficiently.

Enhances Academic Performance: Adequate and regular sleep favorably improves academic performance.

Improved attention and cognitive function lead to higher learning results.

Strengthens Physical Health: Consistent bedtimes are related to higher physical health.

Chronic sleep interruptions may lead to health difficulties, including cardiovascular problems and reduced immunological function.

Promotes Family Harmony: Establishing regular bedtimes may lead to a more peaceful family life.

Predictable sleep regimens assist both persons with ADHD and their caretakers.

Encouraging and sustaining regular bedtimes entails providing a sleep-friendly atmosphere, adding relaxing pre-sleep activities, and cultivating a good bedtime ritual. It is vital to adjust sleep tactics to individual requirements and preferences, realizing that consistency is key to enjoying the full advantages of a good sleep pattern.

Addressing Sleep Challenges

Addressing sleep issues in persons with attention deficit hyperactivity disorder (ADHD) needs a comprehensive strategy that addresses both behavioral and environmental aspects. Here are techniques to assist in managing sleep issues in adults with ADHD:

Establish a Consistent Sleep Schedule: Set a regular sleep routine with consistent bedtimes and wake-up hours, especially on weekends.

Consistency helps regulate circadian cycles and increases the quality of sleep.

Create a Relaxing Bedtime Routine: Develop a relaxing pre-sleep ritual to inform the body that it's time to wind down.

Activities may include reading a book, having a warm bath, or performing relaxation techniques.

Limit Screen Time Before Bed: Reduce exposure to devices (phones, tablets, laptops) at least an hour before sleep.

The blue light emitted from displays may interfere with melatonin generation.

Optimize Sleep Environment: Ensure the bedroom is favorable to sleep by making it cold, dark, and quiet.

Invest in comfy bedding and consider utilizing blackout curtains or white noise devices if required.

Promote Daytime Sun Exposure: Encourage exposure to natural sunshine throughout the day.

Natural light helps regulate the body's internal clock and promotes the sleep-wake cycle.

Limit Stimulants in the Evening: Avoid stimulants such as coffee and nicotine in the hours preceding up to sleep.

These drugs may interfere with the ability to fall asleep.

Regular Physical Activity: Promote frequent physical exercise throughout the day.

Exercise may lead to improved sleep but avoid strenuous activity close to bedtime.

Mindful Eating Habits: Encourage attentive eating habits, and avoid large meals close to sleep.

A modest snack may be suitable if hunger is a barrier to sleep.

Address Anxiety and Stress: Implement stress-reduction strategies, such as deep breathing exercises or mindfulness meditation.

Addressing anxiety and stress may help establish a more peaceful sleep atmosphere.

Limit Naps: If sleeping is unavoidable, restrict it to a short period (20-30 minutes) and avoid napping late in the day.

Excessive daytime napping might interfere with nocturnal sleep.

Consider Sleep Aids with Caution: Consult with healthcare providers before contemplating sleep aids, particularly for persons with ADHD.

Medications should only be used under the advice of a healthcare expert.

Monitor and Adjust: Keep a sleep journal to track sleep habits, noting possible causes or disturbances.

Adjust the sleep regimen as required depending on observations and feedback.

Collaborate with Healthcare Professionals: Consult with healthcare experts, particularly sleep specialists or healthcare providers, to resolve chronic sleep issues. Professionals may examine underlying problems and give specific advice.

Address Coexisting Conditions: Address any concomitant problems that may lead to sleep issues, such as anxiety, depression, or other sleep disorders.

Educate and Involve the Individual: Educate the person about the significance of sleep and engage them in the construction of a sleep pattern.

Encourage their involvement in activities that promote relaxation and better sleep.

Individuals with ADHD may have varied degrees of sleep problems, and a targeted treatment is needed. It's vital to engage closely with healthcare experts, especially sleep specialists, to address underlying concerns and adopt effective measures for increasing sleep quality and length.

Yoga and Meditation for Children

Yoga and meditation may be useful activities for children, particularly those with attention deficit hyperactivity disorder (ADHD). These techniques may assist in enhancing physical well-being, emotional stability, and greater attention. Here are techniques to teach yoga and meditation to children with ADHD:

Yoga for Children with ADHD:

Simple Poses: Introduce simple and pleasant yoga postures appropriate for youngsters.

Examples include Child's Pose, Downward-Facing Dog, Tree Pose, and Butterfly Pose.

Storytelling Yoga: Create a narrative aspect during yoga sessions.

Use inventive storylines to take youngsters through a sequence of postures relevant to the story.

Breathing Exercises: Incorporate easy breathing techniques to promote awareness.

Teach methods like "balloon breath" or "snake breath" to make it entertaining.

Partner Yoga: Explore a couple of yoga postures that entail collaboration and communication.

Partner yoga helps increase social skills and foster trust among youngsters.

Yoga Games: Introduce yoga-themed activities that demand movement and coordination.

Games make the exercise pleasant and participatory.

Music and Movement: Use music to improve the yoga experience.

Encourage rhythmic motions and fluid sequences that match the music.

Sensory Integration: Incorporate sensory aspects into yoga, such as textured mats or props.

Sensory integration may be especially useful for children with ADHD.

Short Sessions: Keep yoga sessions very short, particularly for smaller children.

Aim for sessions that fit their attention spans.

Meditation for Children with ADHD:

Guided Imagery: Use guided imagery to take youngsters through soothing and visualizations.

Encourage them to visualize tranquil settings or engage their senses in a good manner.

Mindful Breathing: Teach fundamental mindful breathing techniques.

Focus on sensations of breath, such as feeling the breath go in and out or counting breaths.

Body Scan Meditation: Guide youngsters through a body scan meditation.

Help them become aware of various regions of their body, fostering relaxation and body awareness.

Loving-Kindness Meditation: Introduce loving-kindness meditation to foster sentiments of compassion.

Encourage youngsters to send happy thoughts and wishes to themselves and others.

Mindful Listening: Practice attentive listening activities.

Use relaxing noises or music and urge youngsters to pay careful attention to the sounds without judgment.

Mindful Walking: Explore mindful walking as a kind of meditation.

Guide youngsters to pay attention to each step and be present in the moment.

Breath Awareness Games: Create games that include breath awareness.

For example, have youngsters blow a feather or a bubble and concentrate on their breath while they do.

Mindfulness Through Art: Integrate mindfulness with creative activities.

Encourage youngsters to concentrate on the process of producing art, encouraging attentive awareness.

Mindfulness Apps for Children: Explore mindfulness applications developed for children.

Some applications feature guided meditations and activities appropriate for various age groups.

When teaching yoga and meditation to children with ADHD, it's crucial to make the practices age-appropriate, fun, and flexible to individual requirements. Additionally, offering a regular and supportive atmosphere supports the development of these skills as useful tools for controlling attention and boosting general well-being.

Stress Reduction Strategies

Stress reduction measures are vital for those with attention deficit hyperactivity disorder (ADHD) since stress may increase symptoms and damage overall well-being. Here are many stress reduction practices that might be beneficial:

Lifestyle Strategies: Regular Physical Activity: Engage in regular physical activity, which has proven advantages for stress reduction.

Activities like walking, jogging, or yoga might be useful.

Adequate Sleep: Prioritize and keep a regular sleep routine.

Ensure that persons with ADHD receive adequate restorative sleep each night.

Healthy Nutrition: Follow a balanced and healthy diet.

Avoid excessive coffee and sugar consumption, since these might lead to higher stress levels.

Time Management: Develop efficient time management skills.

Use tools like calendars and planners to manage chores and decrease the sense of being overwhelmed.

Mindfulness & Meditation: Practice awareness and meditation practices.

Mindful breathing, body scans, and guided meditation may assist in managing stress.

Deep Breathing Exercises: Incorporate deep breathing exercises into regular activities.

Deep, steady breaths may stimulate the body's relaxation response.

Sensory Breaks: Take brief sensory breaks as required. Activities like squeezing a stress ball or using fidget toys may give sensory input and alleviate tension.

Expressive Arts: Engage in expressive arts as a way of stress relief.

Drawing, painting, or writing may serve as creative outlets.

Cognitive Strategies: Positive Self-Talk: Encourage positive self-talk and affirmations.

Replace negative thinking with positive and hopeful remarks.

Cognitive Behavioral Therapy (CBT): Consider treatment, especially Cognitive Behavioral treatment, to address stresses and create coping strategies.

Goal Setting: Break down work into smaller objectives.

Setting realistic and attainable objectives might decrease the sense of being overwhelmed.

Mindfulness-Based Stress Reduction (MBSR): Explore programs or practices that include mindfulness-based stress reduction approaches.

MBSR programs may involve mindfulness meditation and yoga.

Social Support Strategies:

Connect with Others: Cultivate a support network of friends, family, or support groups.

Sharing experiences and getting support may ease stress.

Open Communication: Communicate frankly about tensions and problems.

Discussing problems with others may lead to collaborative problem-solving.

Delegate Tasks: Delegate responsibility when possible.

Sharing responsibilities may minimize the weight and tension associated with various commitments.

Environmental Strategies:

Organize Environment: Maintain an ordered and clutter-free atmosphere.

An organized setting may help to a feeling of control and alleviate stress.

Create a Calming Space: Designate a tranquil location where persons may withdraw when feeling overwhelmed.

Include relaxing items like comfy chairs and peaceful hues.

Minimize Distractions: Minimize distractions in work or study environments.

Creating a focused setting may boost productivity and minimize stress.

Routine and Predictability: Establish routines and regular scheduling.

Predictability may offer a feeling of stability, lowering stress associated with uncertainty.

It's crucial to note that stress reduction tactics may differ across people, and a variety of ways may be most beneficial. Tailoring techniques to the particular requirements and preferences of persons with ADHD is crucial to effectively managing stress and boosting overall well-being. Additionally, obtaining expert counsel from healthcare doctors or mental health professionals may give individualized help.

Chapter 8: Parental Support and Education

Connecting with Other Parents

Connecting with other parents of children with attention deficit hyperactivity disorder (ADHD) is a helpful and encouraging experience. Building a network of parents experiencing similar issues may give emotional empathy, shared ideas, and practical suggestions. Here are methods to connect with other parents:

Local Support Groups: Community Centers and Clinics: Check with local community centers, clinics, or mental health organizations for information on ADHD support groups in your area.

Schools: School counselors or special education departments may provide information regarding parent support groups relating to ADHD.

Online Forums and social media: specialized Websites: Explore specialized websites and forums exclusively focused on ADHD and parenting.

Social Media Communities: Join ADHD parenting communities on sites like Facebook or Reddit, where parents exchange experiences and give support.

Parent-Teacher Associations (PTAs): School Involvement: Attend PTA meetings and school activities to engage with other parents.

Special Education Committees: Participate in special education committees or forums within the school community.

Workshops and Seminars: Local Events: Attend workshops or seminars about ADHD, where you may meet other parents.

Parenting programs: Look for parenting programs that may address themes connected to ADHD.

Therapeutic Programs: Therapy Groups: Inquire about therapy or counseling groups for parents of children with ADHD.

Behavioral Intervention Programs: Programs providing behavioral therapies may give possibilities for parent networking.

Specialized Clinics and Hospitals: Pediatric Clinics: Ask pediatricians or ADHD specialists for information on parent support networks.

Children's Hospitals: Check whether children's hospitals provide support programs for families living with ADHD.

School seminars and Events: Parent Workshops: Attend seminars provided by schools on ADHD and related subjects.

Parenting activities: Participate in school or community parenting activities where you may connect with other parents.

Parenting Conferences: Local Conferences: Attend local conferences or events focusing on parenting and ADHD. Virtual Conferences: Explore virtual conferences that give possibilities for networking.

Parent-Run Organizations: ADHD Parent groups: Some groups are expressly established to help parents of children with ADHD.

Parent-Led Initiatives: Connect with parent-led initiatives or organizations campaigning for ADHD awareness and support.

Local Libraries and Community Centers: Parenting Classes: Check with local libraries or community centers for parenting programs that may appeal to parents of children with ADHD.

Bulletin Boards: Look for bulletin boards or community notices on ADHD-related activities.

Sports and Extracurricular Activities: Team or Club Events: Attend events relating to your child's sports team or extracurricular activities.

casual meetings: Arrange casual meetings with parents during practices or events.

Volunteer Opportunities: Volunteer Programs: Participate in volunteer programs or community service where you may meet other parents.

Parent-Led Initiatives: Get active in parent-led initiatives focusing on ADHD awareness.

School Support Staff: Special Education Coordinators: Contact special education coordinators or support staff at your child's school for information about parent support networks.

School Counselors: School counselors may offer information regarding parent organizations or services.

Create Your Group: Organize meetings: Initiate local meetings or gatherings for parents of children with ADHD.

Online Platforms: Create an online community or forum for parents to connect and exchange resources.

Building ties with other parents gives a useful support system and a venue for exchanging experiences and techniques. Whether via local clubs, internet forums, or community events, interacting with other parents experiencing similar issues may add to a feeling of understanding and empowerment.

Sharing Experiences and Strategies

Sharing experiences and techniques with other parents of children with attention deficit hyperactivity disorder

(ADHD) may be enormously valuable. The sharing of thoughts, problems, and successful ways develop a feeling of understanding and camaraderie. Here are methods to exchange experiences and techniques within a supportive community:

Participate in Support Groups:

a. **Join Local Groups:** Attend local ADHD support groups where parents congregate to discuss their experiences.

b. **Online Forums:** Participate in online forums or social media groups devoted to ADHD parenting.

Storytelling and Personal Narratives:

a. **Share Personal Stories:** Open about your story as a parent of a kid with ADHD.

b. **Narrate achievements and problems:** Narrate both achievements and problems to create a balanced picture.

Organize Sharing Sessions:

a. **Facilitate Discussions:** Organize or participate in sharing sessions when parents take turns explaining their experiences.

b. **Themed Sessions:** Have sessions focusing on certain issues, such as behavior management or school advocacy.

Create a Blog or Journal:

a. **Document Your Journey:** Start a blog or diary detailing your experiences parenting a kid with ADHD.

b. **Include Strategies:** Share solutions that have worked for your family.

Collaborative Problem-Solving:

a. **Discuss Challenges:** Engage in conversations regarding difficulties you're experiencing.

b. **Seek Input:** Encourage people to contribute their techniques and thoughts for solving similar issues.

Positive Reinforcement Stories:

a. **Share Success Stories:** Highlight instances when positive reinforcement or tactics led to favorable results.

b. **Celebrate Milestones:** Celebrate milestones and successes, no matter how minor.

Regular Check-Ins:

a. **Establish Regular Check-Ins:** Create a pattern for regular check-ins where parents may inform one another of their experiences.

b. **Virtual Meetings:** Utilize virtual meetings for check-ins, enabling accessibility for everyone.

Resource Sharing:

a. **Share Helpful Resources:** Pass along good articles, books, or online resources that have been beneficial. Educational items: Share items that have helped you better understand ADHD and parenting practices.

Peer Mentoring:

a. **Establish mentoring:** Establish peer mentoring programs throughout the community.

b. **Experienced Parents Supporting Newcomers:** Experienced parents may give direction and support to those newer to the path.

Parenting seminars:

a. **Teach Workshops:** If comfortable, teach seminars on certain themes, providing your skills and experiences.

b. **Attend seminars:** Attend seminars held by other parents to learn different views.

Interactive Online Platforms:

a. **Engage in Discussions:** Participate actively in online venues where debates are welcomed.

b. **Respond to Queries:** Offer help by responding to queries or concerns from other parents.

Social Events and Meetings:

a. **Informal Gatherings:** Organize or attend informal meetings where parents may exchange experiences in a relaxed atmosphere.

b. **Coffee meetings:** Schedule coffee meetings or playdates to promote informal talks.

Create a Supportive climate:

a. **Non-Judgmental Environment:** Foster a non-judgmental climate where all parents feel comfortable sharing their experiences.

b. **Encourage Openness:** Encourage openness and ensure confidentiality within the group.

Feedback and Advice:

a. **Seek Feedback:** Seek feedback on your tactics or approaches.

b. **Offer counsel:** Provide counsel based on your experiences, always with the awareness that each kid is unique.

Celebrate Differences:

a. **Acknowledge Diverse Experiences:** Recognize that each family's experience is unique.

b. **Learn from Differences:** Embrace and learn from the variety of experiences within the community.

Sharing experiences and techniques within a supportive network of parents living with ADHD generates a rich tapestry of insights and resources. It helps establish a feeling of connection, understanding, and empowerment as parents manage the specific difficulties involved with parenting a kid with ADHD.

Keeping up with Research and Resources

Staying updated on the latest research and resources linked to attention deficit hyperactivity disorder (ADHD) is vital for parents looking to help their children successfully.

Here are techniques to stay up with research and access helpful resources:

Online Research Platforms:

a. **PubMed:** Explore PubMed, a comprehensive database of scientific articles, to access the latest research on ADHD.

b. **Google Scholar:** Use Google Scholar to uncover research publications, conference papers, and patents linked to ADHD.

Professional Organizations:

a. **American Academy of Child and Adolescent Psychiatry (AACAP):** AACAP offers information, recommendations, and updates on ADHD research.

b. **Children and Adults with Attention-Deficit/Hyperactivity Disorder (CHADD):** CHADD provides information, webinars, and resources for parents.

Educational Websites:

a. **National Institute of Mental Health (NIMH):** NIMH offers information about ADHD research, treatment alternatives, and clinical trials.

b. **Centers for Disease Control and Prevention (CDC):** The CDC provides educational resources and updates on ADHD.

c. **Subscription to publications:** Subscribe to Journals: Consider subscribing to relevant publications, such as the Journal of Attention Disorders, to obtain the newest research immediately.

d. Online Journal Access: Many journals allow online access, giving a simple method to remain informed.

e. Research Newsletters: Subscribe to Newsletters: Sign up for newsletters from trustworthy organizations working on ADHD research.

University Research Updates: Universities regularly distribute newsletters summarizing current research results.

Participation in Clinical studies:

a. **ClinicalTrials.gov:** Explore ClinicalTrials.gov to gather information on active clinical studies linked to ADHD.

b. **Discuss with Healthcare professionals:** Consult with healthcare professionals about prospective involvement in clinical trials.

Social media and Online Forums:

a. **Follow Researchers:** Follow scholars, institutions, and organizations on social media sites for real-time information.

b. **Engage in Forums:** Participate in online forums or groups where parents discuss the latest study results and exchange information.

Library Resources:

   a. **University Libraries:** Access university libraries, where you may obtain books, journals, and research papers on ADHD.

   b. **Public Libraries:** Public libraries typically contain materials about ADHD for parents.

Attend Conferences and Workshops:

   a. **ADHD Conferences:** Attend conferences and workshops focused on ADHD research and parenting strategies.

   a. **Parenting Seminars:** Participate in seminars organized by healthcare institutions or parenting organizations.

Healthcare Provider Guidance:

   a. **Regular Consultations:** Schedule regular consultations with your child's healthcare provider to discuss the latest research findings.

   b. **Ask for Recommendations:** Request suggestions for credible resources and updates.

Webinars and Online Courses:

a. **Online Webinars:** Attend webinars conducted by ADHD experts and organizations.

b. **Online Courses:** Enroll in online courses that give in-depth information about ADHD research and treatment.

Community Resources:

a. **Local Support Groups:** Join local support groups where parents may exchange the latest study results.

b. **Community programs:** Attend programs given by community centers or mental health groups.

School Collaboration:

a. **Collaborate with School Professionals:** Work closely with teachers and school professionals who may have access to educational materials and research updates.

b. **School Presentations:** Attend presentations or seminars provided by the school about ADHD.

Podcasts and Audiobooks:

a. **ADHD Podcasts:** Listen to podcasts that offer conversations on ADHD research and parenting practices.

b. **Audiobooks:** Explore audiobooks that discuss the newest breakthroughs in ADHD research.

Parenting Apps and Technology:

a. **Apps with Research Updates:** Use parenting apps that give frequent updates on ADHD research.

b. **Online Platforms:** Explore online platforms that employ technology to give relevant information.

Staying informed needs, a proactive approach, and employing a mix of these tactics may help parents discover the latest research and information on ADHD. Regular contact with healthcare specialists and involvement in supportive networks further help the knowledge and treatment of ADHD-related issues.

Advocating for Your Child

Advocating for your kid with attention deficit hyperactivity disorder (ADHD) is a key role that parents play in ensuring their child's scholastic and emotional needs are addressed. Here are ways for successful advocacy:

Educate Yourself:

a. **Understand ADHD:** Gain a full grasp of ADHD, including its symptoms, problems, and strengths.

b. **Learn about Rights:** Familiarize yourself with the legal rights and accommodations accessible to kids with ADHD in school settings.

Build a Support Team:

a. **Healthcare Professionals:** Establish cooperation with your child's healthcare professionals, including physicians, psychiatrists, and therapists.

b. **Educators:** Collaborate with teachers, special education specialists, and school administrators.

c. **Support Groups:** Join support groups to interact with other parents and exchange experiences.

Document Your Child's Needs:

a. **Keep Records:** Maintain a record of your child's ADHD-related struggles, successes, and any pertinent discussions with experts.

b. Request Assessments: If required, seek educational and psychological exams to better understand your child's strengths and needs.

Develop a Parenting Plan:

a. Establish Routines: Work with your child's healthcare professionals and educators to build routines that promote your child's achievement.

b. Behavioral tactics: Implement evidence-based behavioral tactics at home to promote good behavior.

Communication with Educators:

a. Open Dialogue: Maintain open contact with your child's teachers and school workers.

b. Regular Updates: Request regular updates on your child's growth and well-being.

Participate in Individualized Education Program (IEP) Meetings:

a. Attend Meetings: Attend IEP meetings to actively participate in the formulation and revision of your child's educational plan.

b. **Express Concerns:** Voice your concerns, share ideas about your kid, and participate in creating suitable objectives.

Know Your Child's Rights:

a. **Legal rights:** Familiarize yourself with the Individuals with Disabilities Education Act (IDEA) and Section 504 of the Rehabilitation Act, which offers legal rights for students with disabilities.

b. **Accommodations:** Understand the accommodations and services your kid is entitled to in the school context.

Effective Communication:

a. **Clear and Concise Messages:** Clearly explain your child's needs, talents, and problems.

b. **Use Positive Language:** Frame talks positively and constructively, highlighting your child's potential.

Collaborate on Behavioral Plans:

a. **Positive Behavioral Interventions:** Work with the school to establish positive behavioral interventions that correspond with your child's needs.

b. Consistency Across Settings: Ensure consistency in behavioral methods between home and school.

Stay Informed about School Policies:

a. **Know School Policies:** Understand the regulations and processes connected to ADHD within the educational system.

b. **Advocate for Policy Changes:** Advocate for changes if you find areas that may be improved.

Seek extra Support Services:

a. **Specialized Services:** If required, advocate for extra support services such as occupational therapy, counseling, or social skills training.

b. **Outside Resources:** Explore community resources and services that may supplement your child's educational and emotional requirements.

Promote Self-Advocacy Skills:

a. **Teach Advocacy Skills:** Encourage your kid to recognize their own needs and advocate for themselves as they progress.

b. **Self-Expression:** Foster an atmosphere where your kid feels comfortable expressing their needs to educators and peers.

Address Bullying and Stigma:

a. **Anti-Bullying Measures:** Advocate for anti-bullying measures within the school to provide a safe and supportive environment.

b. **Educate Peers:** Collaborate with the school to educate peers about ADHD, decreasing stigma and increasing empathy.

Stay Engaged in Professional Development:

a. **Attend Workshops and Seminars:** Participate in workshops or seminars on ADHD advocacy and parenting.

b. **Stay Updated:** Keep up with the newest information about ADHD research and instructional solutions.

Know When to Seek Legal Advice:

a. **Legal Consultation:** If you experience chronic difficulty in acquiring reasonable accommodations, talk with an education attorney to explore your legal alternatives.

Effective advocacy takes continual communication, teamwork, and a dedication to ensuring that your child's specific needs are acknowledged and fulfilled within the school system. Stay educated, create strong connections with educators, and enable your kids to become self-advocate as they grow.

Printed in Great Britain
by Amazon

37098260R00096